Feminist Thinkers and
the Demands of Femininity

Feminist Thinkers and
the Demands of Femininity

The Lives and Work of Intellectual Women

Lori Jo Marso

Routledge
Taylor & Francis Group
New York   London

Routledge is an imprint of the
Taylor & Francis Group, an informa business

Note: Chapter 5 was first published in *Feminist Theory* 4, no. 3 (December 2003) and is republished in *Feminist Interpretations of Emma Goldman*, edited by Penny Weiss and Loretta Kensinger, Re-reading the Canon Series (College Park: Pennsylvania State University Press, 2007). Chapter 6 is included in *Simone de Beauvoir's Political Thinking*, edited by Lori Jo Marso and Patricia Moynagh (Champaign: University of Illinois Press, 2006).

Routledge
Taylor & Francis Group
270 Madison Avenue
New York, NY 10016

Routledge
Taylor & Francis Group
2 Park Square
Milton Park, Abingdon
Oxon OX14 4RN

© 2006 by Taylor and Francis Group, LLC
Routledge is an imprint of Taylor & Francis Group, an Informa business

Printed in the United States of America on acid-free paper
10 9 8 7 6 5 4 3 2 1

International Standard Book Number-10: 0-415-97927-7 (Softcover) 0-415-97926-9 (Hardcover)
International Standard Book Number-13: 978-0-415-97927-6 (Softcover) 978-0-415-97926-9 (Hardcover)
Library of Congress Card Number 2005035264

Library of Congress Cataloging-in-Publication Data

Marso, Lori Jo.
   Feminist thinkers and the demands of femininity : the lives and work of intellectual women / Lori Jo Marso.
      p. cm.
   Includes bibliographical references.
      ISBN 0-415-97926-9 (hb) -- ISBN 0-415-97927-7 (pb)
      1. Feminists--Biography. 2. Feminists--Social conditions. 3. Feminism. 4. Femininity. 5. Women's studies--Biographical methods. I. Title.

HQ1123.M35 2006
305.42092'2--dc22   2005035264

Visit the Taylor & Francis Web site at
http://www.taylorandfrancis.com

and the Routledge Web site at
http://www.routledge-ny.com

Table of Contents

v

Preface

Feminism, Femininity, and Solidarity

A woman is free when she chooses to signify her belonging to the female
sex, well knowing it is not an object of choice.

Milan Women's Bookstore Collective (1990, 138)

Feminist biographies and autobiographies have always fascinated and
inspired me. The ones I find especially intriguing explore the life
circumstances of feminist theorists whom I initially came to know
through their political and philosophical work. As I started to read
feminist autobiographies with more serious questions in mind, I was
drawn in by their struggles, both personal and political, to live their
lives in the way they desired, maybe even in the feminist ways they had
argued for in their theories. I also became curious about how society's
definition of these feminists as *women* constrained and enabled their
own sense of themselves and their political alliances.

Within this book, I read each feminist's theoretical and political
essays and texts alongside their memoirs, letters, and autobiographical
novels. By way of this juxtaposition, I probe their reflections on

whether they each, individually, felt able to live their own lives in what they considered to be feminist ways. Sometimes I find that gender norms, theorized in this work as the demands of femininity, prevented these women from living the lives they would have desired. What do we learn from discovering that our feminist mothers were not always able to create and inhabit feminist ways of living?

A contemporary reviewer of biographical scholarship on Mary Wollstonecraft remarks that "today's feminist scholars like their heroines simple, like them practicing what they preach and preaching what they (the scholars, that is) preach too" (Nehring 2002, 61). This reviewer taps into an intense anxiety feminists have about revealing any weaknesses or shortcomings in the lives of feminist heroines for fear of being called misogynists themselves. Nevertheless, if we are willing only to present the lives of feminist thinkers playing out consistently with the goals described within their theories, we lose our opportunity to learn about, and be inspired by, the historical struggles of feminists to define alternative ways of living. We also lose our chance to appreciate the enormous obstacles placed in the path of such feminists who, through their lived experiences, challenged their society's gender norms.

The thinkers I choose to explore take up the question of feminism in ways that simultaneously chart the material and the existential conditions of femininity. Though each feminist faced significant and sometimes immoveable obstacles within her lifetime, each woman's lived experience challenged the demands of femininity prevalent within her own cultural, historical, class, and racially constituted location. The work of these feminist thinkers reveals that femininity is always articulated, and struggled against, as a situation. Women find themselves within structures, not of their making, that produce and assign meaning to their bodies and desires. At the same time, however, feminist women, such as the ones whose work and lives I attend to in this book, constantly push up against and thus expose these confines by expressing their existential paths toward individuality.

This work came to sustain me during times when feminism, as we knew it, was suffering. In spite of signs of healthy feminist activism on local and global levels, as well as the indisputable need for feminist theorizing and practice in an increasingly inequitable world, we are said to live in "post-feminist" times. Students on my campus, for example, most likely no different from their counterparts on other campuses, often subscribe to a belief that at least in this country feminist battles have been fought and won and the advances made by feminism solidified. In accordance with this line of thought, the only feminist work left to be done is of the sort enacted by the "W Stands for Women" George W. Bush administration: bringing "freedom" at the barrel of a gun to "helpless" women in places such as Afghanistan and Iraq.

Within this "post-feminist" political condition, popular and journalistic culture continuously portrays the ill effects feminism has wreaked on contemporary women. The image of burned-out, infertile women suffering from a man shortage or unable to have it all in the way that feminism promised comes at us from every quarter. From all political perspectives, we are told that what women were promised by feminism is impossible and that the expansion of our desires is at the heart of our misery. Clearly, whether we are really miserable or just being told that feminism has made us miserable by fostering our need for both public and private fulfillment, the question of how to juggle public and private goals—how to live fulfilling professional as well as personal lives—is a question that merits urgent attention. To be promised the possibility of having it all, and then to have those possibilities closed off, puts women at the heart of an unfinished revolution, with all the frustrations and disappointment that entails.

Because feminism has lost its political salience within mainstream discourse, the fact that women suffer disproportionately within our current conservative political environment goes unmentioned, if not unnoticed altogether. The lack of affordable health care, the erosion of Social Security benefits, the dearth of quality and affordable child-care options, the severe restrictions on welfare, the threat of dismantlement of *Roe v. Wade*, and the diversion of funds from domestic use to military misadventures all affect women far more directly and adversely than any other segment of the population. All women are the losers in this political climate, and we need to speak politically, as women, to address these issues.

The political context I just described cries out for a feminist response, yet feminism is riddled with internal divisions that prevent a unified front. Criticisms of second-wave feminist theorizing, which focused on the diversity of women's experiences based in our social, economic, racial, and sexual identities, exposed the paradoxical position in which we feminists have always found ourselves. Can we speak as women without reinscribing women as an oppressive social category? With numerous feminist voices speaking out from a variety of specific locations, the idea that we might speak in a unified voice has seemed increasingly impossible.

To negotiate this impasse, I interpret Simone de Beauvoir's *The Second Sex* within a political framework. In this founding text,

Beauvoir asks how we might discover who women are, leaving that question wide open rather than predetermined. She then proceeds to the more pressing existential concern: How might we women come together to speak and act politically? Rather than locate women as a biological or a social category or as a group possessing any special kind of knowledge, Beauvoir asks us instead to think of women as human beings frustrated in our attempts to articulate and realize our desires. Beauvoir criticizes the notion of the eternal feminine, a mythical category that works to subsume women under its umbrella despite our highly particular and dazzlingly complex locations and identities. As an alternative to seeing women as sharing any essential qualities, a particular kind of knowledge, or a specified identity, we might focus instead on the political potential of working together in alliances. My reading of Beauvoir illuminates this alternative way to constitute women politically. Were we to think of ourselves as feminists who share the desire for freedom and enhanced possibilities, we might join together to challenge the social interpretation of our existence.

My reading of the lives and work of individual feminist intellectuals is inspired by Beauvoir's writings about particular women in *The Second Sex*. Through my exploration of personal and philosophical writings by these thinkers, I articulate a specifically feminist intervention into current political debates. The feminist thinkers I study share a feminist politics promising general emancipation and embracing liberating visions while recognizing and documenting the social, cultural, and economic constraints under which we currently—or as each feminist writes within her historical moment—live. Specifically, I explore the writings of historical and contemporary feminist thinkers on questions concerning how changing definitions of femininity affect women's possibilities for living our lives in accordance with feminist ideals.

Some of the most pressing questions these feminists raise are ones that prior to the women's movement would have been considered private matters. They ask about the politics of romantic love, constructions of sexuality and deviance, the dictates and material conditions of marriage, the demands of monogamy for women, women's "choice" to have children and/or to do "flexible" work in the home or nontraditional work in the labor market. In short, they ask how our most intimate relationships, our understandings of ourselves and our worth, and our potential contribution to society all are constructed within and throughout the social definitions and demands of femininity. Their work reveals that femininity is a cultural and material force through which women must negotiate their subjectivity. Femininity manifests itself specifically, constituted by class, race, and political and historical circumstances to differently enable and constrain the lives of all women.

My method links women's lives within our maternal and feminist inheritance. The chapters are connected by my efforts to link women together as feminists. To claim belonging in a community of feminists, we must recognize our inheritance from a feminist genealogy of predecessors, as well as from the mothers who raised us. And though we are constituted socially and politically in categories that mark our specific locations of racial and class difference, we might undo them via challenging the demands of femininity.

Charting a feminist genealogy, I look to the lives of our feminist predecessors to assess whether and how feminists—and subsequently all women—might come to redefine the meanings assigned to being and becoming women. Reading the stories of these women's lives in the context of their feminist work reveals the tremendous hurdles we face but also the urgent necessity we must bring toward enacting political transformation.

What I find is that the demands of femininity constrain our attempts to become women differently. In engaging with the historical and contemporary lived dilemmas of feminists, we make a political claim to membership in a genealogy of women. Reading their struggles for freedom sympathetically, I argue, teaches us to read our own dilemmas as a shared effort to articulate and act on desires. By making other feminists our privileged interlocutors, I hope we can come together as women in political coalition. Only then can we transgress and undo norms of femininity to free ourselves to be women in ways heretofore unimagined.

Acknowledgments

I am delighted to finaly be able to publicly acknowledge my debt to my many friends and colleagues who made it possible for me to write this book. First, I want to thank the theorists who gather each year for the Feminist Pre-Conference of the Western Political Science Association. Within this group, Martha Ackelsberg, Mary Bellhouse, Kathy Ferguson, Michaele Ferguson, Mary Hawkesworth, Laurie Naranch, and Elizabeth Wingrove each made helpful comments on drafts of specific chapters or helped me to clarify my thoughts in conversation.

At Union College, I am lucky to be surrounded by a core of wonderfully supportive friends and colleagues. Michelle Chilcoat devoted incredible time and energy to this project by reading almost every chapter, offering probing and thoughtful criticism and stimulating my thinking with her intelligent insights and questions. Andy Feffer read many chapters, provided me with new ways to think of my project, and assured me that it was indeed an intellectual history. Andrea Foroughi guided me on historical context for my work on Ida B. Wells and Emma Goldman. Charlotte Eyerman carefully read and talked with me about early versions of the chapters on Mary Wollstonecraft, Germaine de Staël, and Simone de Beauvoir. Richard Fox endured many hours listening to me verbalize both my worries about and great hopes for this manuscript. Lita Camacho-Platero was constantly supportive and had great insights for the chapter on Emma Goldman. Martha Huggins and Brenda Wineapple, two wonderful senior colleagues, have supported my work and also inspired me as engaged, critical, and generous feminist intellectuals. I also want to thank my students in seminars on women intellectuals, twentieth-century women philosophers, and feminist theory. Their questions and honest appraisal of our conversations greatly benefited my writing. These students pushed me to think more deeply while enthusiastically sharing my passion for studying the lives and work of feminist intellectuals.

I received a writing grant from the National Endowment for the Humanities to begin this book in 2000–01 and used the time to live in Seville, Spain, with my family and to write three of the early chapters. During my sabbatical year from Union College, 2003–04, I continued my writing in Oaxaca, Mexico, and finished a first draft of the whole manuscript. In Spain and in Mexico, I met friends who sustained my work at a time when I was away from my usual intellectual community. Geoff and Rosemary Murray, Mary Alice Soriero, Mary Ann Garrett, and Elizabeth Bell became good friends during those years.

In addition, my friend Victoria Wohl read an early version of the entire manuscript and offered insightful and encouraging comments that greatly improved subsequent drafts. Linda Zerilli read chapter 6 and spoke with me about how I might discuss Beauvoir's

contribution to contemporary feminism. I thank Kimberly Guinta, my editor at Routledge, for believing in this project, working with me so patiently, and giving her time and expertise so generously at every stage. The anonymous reviewers of this manuscript were sympathetic, probing, and critical, and their comments helped me to write the best book I could.

I have been fortunate to have had many opportunities to present parts of this work to groups of women of older generations. On one occasion after presenting the chapter on Goldman, an attractive woman in her seventies approached me to ask how I would advise her to go on with her life after having reminded her of all she had lost. I was surprised by the honesty of her comment and urged her to explain. She offered that she had taken "women's courses" in college, but had "abandoned all that" to get married and raise three children. Her husband had recently died, but she shared that long before that, something in her had died. Having just lectured on Goldman's critique of marriage and her emphasis on women's freedom, especially the need for women to voice and pursue their creative dreams, I was pretty sure I knew what this older woman meant. I have talked about this troubling encounter with my students in subsequent years to urge them to consider it as a warning. Beauvoir says that because women are always defined in relation to men, we are continually tempted to take the "easy slopes" and are socially rewarded for doing so. By this she means that it remains incredibly difficult, as well as socially and politically risky, for women to articulate our desires and to chart our own paths toward engagement with the world. Over many years, I have participated in ongoing intimate and intellectual conversations with friends—particularly my dear friends Marla Brettschneider and

Patricia Moynagh—about what it means to resist the easy slopes. I have been inspired by the life choices of many of my close friends—in their careers, their travels, and their values—that are often well outside the mainstream. To seek these challenges and to try to think clearly about our political responsibilities is to claim freedom in the way Beauvoir articulated. It is to leave the comfortable and the expected and to try to live differently. I am especially grateful to Pat and Marla for these conversations and experiments in challenging conventions that helped me to write this book as well as to think about how to live my own life.

My family has more than supported my desires and choices; they have often made them possible. On one level, this book is about acknowledging our debt to feminist mothers—of all kinds—to free ourselves to forge feminist coalitions and relationships with each other. In this spirit of gratitude and reciprocity, I want to thank my mother, Jo Marso. As I entered my adult years, my mother became a source of support for me in my efforts to interpret and reinvent femininity and especially motherhood. I thank my mother for her willingness to acknowledge that there are many ways to be a mother, many ways to show love, many different ways to be a woman. During the year my partner and I had a long-distance relationship, for example, I often needed to "abandon" my young crying son to hours of institutional daycare and then hire a teenage babysitter to stay with him in the evening as I frantically prepared for classes. Many of these nights I called my mother in tears to report on the latest ways in which I was failing as a mother—how it turned out that though I thought I could do it, I had discovered I was unable to balance my responsibilities as a professor with my life as a single mother. Each time my mother would calmly assure me that my son, Lucas, was fine; that he remained pretty much undamaged, whole, and loved; and that my life and goals were important too. When my daughter, Luci, was only ten days old and I traveled across the country for a job interview, again my mother reassured me it was a good decision. I did, however, start to wonder about this later on, when at the tender and presumably innocent age of three months, my defiant daughter would punish me by turning her head swiftly away from me to look lovingly toward her father, refusing to acknowledge my return from yet another academic conference. My daughter now loves these stories and finds them useful to retell, humorously and in her own style, when she wants to claim that I am not the most devoted of mothers.

Providing continual surprises, expectations, and needs, Lucas and Luci Lobe are a welcome source of challenge and daily joy. As they develop, grow, and change, I thank them for examining their own lives in the spirit in which their father and I are raising them. Lucas recently wondered if seeing an American flag on the lawn of a girl he fancied might be a "real relationship killer," and Luci practices passive resistance (turning into active resistance against her parents) and thoughtfully articulates what it means to her to be a feminist. I also sincerely thank my father, Tom Marso, for being the kind of parent he is: always there for me and willing to grow and change himself as well as to foster my growth. My dad is one of my most persistent combatants and, at the same time, my most loyal fan. I also thank Jeff, Rita, and Lynn Marso, and Geoffrey, Guthrie, and Danielle Gray-Lobe for their love and their belief in me. Each member of my family offers his or her own distinctive challenges and models of ways of living. They are an eclectic and loving support network. Our dogs, Mole Negro and Emma, provide loads of unwavering support, too, expressed through their slavish devotion and wagging tails.

Finally, I dedicate this book to my partner, Tom Lobe. Tom read each chapter more times than either he or I would like to remember. He was my closest interlocutor for every idea and came up with many of his own that are articulated in these pages and wrongly ascribed to me. Most important, Tom is my best friend, my lover, and my partner; he has always made and continues to make all my dreams possible.

1. Feminist Genealogies

Connecting Women's Lives

Carolyn Kay Steedman (1986) expresses the difficulty feminists have thinking and working with genealogies.[1] Speaking of her own mother, Steedman says, "My refusal of my mother's body was, I think, a recognition of the problem that my own physical presence represented to her; and at the same time it was a refusal of the inexorable nature of that difficulty, that it would *go on* like that, that I would become her, and come to reproduce the circumstances of our straitened unsatisfying life" (pp. 94, 95).

The feminist daughter's impulse is to refuse the mother's body, wanting nothing to do with it out of fear of becoming her mother. She sees the demands of femininity written on her mother's body and exemplified in the way her mother has had to live out her life. Christine Stansell (2000, 246, 247) documents that "the desire for a life different from the mother's was one of the great psychological themes of this generation on both sides of the Atlantic" and so dominated the conditions of female modernism that the disavowal of the mother came "almost to be a trademark." Within the literature of the female moderns, feelings about mothers were "personal, cutting, reproachful" (ibid.).

The same can be said for the feelings and writings exhibited by feminist thinkers approaching the work of feminist mothers. The profound ambivalence when confronting the mother is especially poignant, it seems, when feminists look at the lives of our feminist mothers. For in spite of intellectual achievements and political commitments, each feminist thinker that I study still has had to live out her life within societies that define femininity, and what it is to be a woman, in ways that limit women's and even each feminist's own substantive choices.

Recognizing Our Mothers

Rosi Braidotti (1994, 207) calls feminist genealogy "the process of thinking backwards through the work of other women...genealogies are politically informed counter-memories which keep us connected to the experiences and the speaking voices of some of the women whose resistance is for us a source of support and inspiration." Luce Irigaray (1993a, 19) calls on feminists to embrace such genealogical work. "Let us not forget," she argues, "that we already have a history, that certain women, despite all the cultural obstacles, have made their mark on history and all too often have been forgotten by us." Irigaray stresses the importance of genealogy in her emphasis on mother–daughter relationships. She argues that we must recognize our mothers, both literal and figurative, to forge political relationships of sisterhood. Irigaray demands that we move beyond the Freudian scene whereby the girl must turn away from her mother as the necessary condition for the assumption of femininity. As Irigary puts it, "Because we have been exiled into the house of our husbands, it is easy to forget the special quality of our female genealogy; we might even come to deny it. Let us try to situate ourselves within that female genealogy so that we can win and hold on to our identity" (p. 19).

Drucilla Cornell (2002, xviii) adds that marking a female genealogy as "intergenerational" does not limit the investigation to relationships between biological mothers and daughters or even to relationships between living women. In her work on genealogy, Cornell inspires links between women within maternal as well as political genealogies. Although we can never fully know the true story of another woman's life, we can open up a dialogue wherein women might encounter difference between and among women, identifying how each woman has tried to carve a space for her own life beyond the limits of gender identity. To politically chart the ways the demands of femininity have constrained women's lives in various and specific locations is a first step toward loosening the grip these demands make on our lives. Just knowing about how other women have struggled with the dictates of femininity within their own locations can ease the loneliness Audre Lorde expresses (1982, 176): "I remember how being young and Black and gay and lonely felt. A lot of it was fine, feeling I had the truth and the light and the key, but a lot of it was purely hell. There were no mothers, no sisters, no heroes. We had to do it alone, like our sister Amazons, the riders on the loneliest outposts of the kingdom of Dahomey."

My own genealogical work is driven by a continuing curiosity about how women whose political and feminist thought I admire struggled to live out their feminist dreams. Germaine de Staël, Mary Wollstonecraft, Emma Goldman, and Simone de Beauvoir, all of whom could be classified as feminist mothers or canonical feminist theorists, each explicitly explored the links, contradictions, ambiguities, and fissures between the social and cultural demands of femininity and the desires they expressed as intellectual, feminist women. Digging more deeply into the lives and work of these women, I became increasingly fascinated by how each of them thought about their own lives and their various roles as philosophers, activists, writers, feminists, and women. I wondered how, for each of these exemplary women, thinking as a feminist might have been in tension with, or challenged by, being a woman, and how they negotiated these conflicts and tensions in their lives.

Exploring the tensions, contradictions, and gaps in the intersections between living as a woman and thinking as a feminist in the lives of these feminist theorists led me to the genres of biography, autobiography, and epistolary exchange. One of the first questions that jumped out at me when I began this book was one whose answer I naively hoped would illuminate for me how to better manage my own life: Where did they find the time to do all that writing? In addition to plays, letters, memoirs, and innumerable essays and political analyses, Germaine de Staël bequeathed to us three volumes numbering over a thousand pages on the events of the French Revolution, a treatise on literature in relation to social institutions, a study on Germany considered one of the first extensive works of comparative literature, and two lengthy novels portraying the dilemmas of the independent woman.[2] Janet Todd and Marilyn Butler's collected volumes on the work of Mary Wollstonecraft likewise displays her range and productivity: seven volumes numbering thousands of pages on politics, religion, revolution, the education of daughters, as well as novels, short stories, and letters. In addition to *The Second Sex*, Simone de Beauvoir also wrote four novels including *The Mandarins*, a multivolume autobiography, a treatise on her travels through America, and the philosophical *Ethics of Ambiguity*. And finally, along with *Living My Life* (her two-volume autobiography), *My Disillusionment in Russia*, and scores of political pamphlets, speeches, and essays on a range of topics, Emma Goldman wrote hundreds of letters to her friends and comrades. The sheer volume of work produced by these four feminist authors could keep a scholar like me forever trapped in the role of attentive reader.

The awe invoked in response to the volume of the written word, however, is subsequently replaced by interpretive panic. As feminist readers, how should we connect to, understand, and utilize the presentation of the lives and work of our feminist mothers? Within this book, I demonstrate that our feminist heroines lived extremely complex lives indeed. They were drawn, often too powerfully, into love affairs—some unwise and scandalous; they had great difficulty balancing career and family; when they attempted to redefine meanings of family, love, and intimacy by living their lives outside the norm, they were forced to face society's disdain; and in light of these struggles, each feminist occasionally submitted to disillusionment and despair. In truth, these women's lives sometimes clashed with their theories. What they wanted for themselves as women was complicated and difficult to achieve, but at every moment in writing theory and in living politics they were redefining the meanings of being a woman in ways that were at odds with their historical moment and cultural location.

Femininity As Situation

When studying the lives of our mothers—those who raised us as well as those we consider mothers of feminism—one of the first things we notice is that femininity is not an eternal, essential, or stable construct. Femininity operates as a gender norm, which we as subjects are constituted through and conditioned by, bound up with specific ideas of race, class, sexuality and all aspects of what Beauvoir calls situation. For example, as we will see in Chapter 2, the norms of femininity for black and white women in nineteenth-century America varied enormously. A white woman who failed to live up to the nineteenth-century cult of true womanhood was subject to oppression as a "deviant" or "insufficient" woman. A black woman, in contrast, was considered wholly unintelligible in terms of these same norms.

Nineteeth-century black women, seen as less than human and subject as a race to "a history of sexual exploitation, were outside the realm of *womanhood* and its prerogatives" (Giddings 1984, 49, my emphasis). The ways that femininity inhered differently for white and black women led to different political responses. Paula Giddings (ibid.) explains that black women saw no distinction between domesticity and political action, for example, and were willing to combine these two ideals. Radical white women, in contrast, condemned domesticity outright because for them, domesticity was too closely associated with the notions of submission, piety, and purity central to the ideal of the cult of true womanhood.

Central to my argument throughout this book is that notions of femininity constrain the lives of women within their specific locations and must be subject to our critical scrutiny. Opening up the demands of femininity to examination across women's lives, starting with the lives of our feminist mothers, provides the possibility for critical comparisons concerning the relational nature of difference. This kind of scrutiny reveals that women's lives are linked by interlocking systems of oppression. As Elsa Barkley Brown (1997, 275) observes: "Middle-class women live the lives they do precisely because working-class women live the lives they do." We need to acknowledge how each of us is differently situated within systems of oppression to forge coalitions that seek to ameliorate these interlocking structures. Linda Zerilli (2005) describes political action of this sort as an enactment of our ability to make judgments and to express our freedom. Zerilli adds that "in the judgment, we affirm our freedom and discover what we have—and do not have—in common" (p. 163). To make these critical comparisons and to find what we do and do not have in common, we must consciously recognize ourselves as belonging to a community of women. The Milan Women's Bookstore Collective (1990, 114) expresses this belonging as an assertion of sexual difference, "part and parcel of [women's] humanity," and central to women's freedom. When we place ourselves in community with other women, we can acknowledge disparity in and across our lives. To begin the process of unlocking oppressive structural conditions through strategic coalitions, we must recognize our sexed existence within a female genealogy and acknowledge our specific location within structures of gender, race, class, and the global economy. By speaking, acting, and judging as feminists we can begin to work together in political coalitions.

I demonstrate that despite the differences in the lives of the women studied in this book, they had much in common. Moreover, the dilemmas these feminist intellectuals faced illuminate our own contemporary dilemmas. And finally, they allow us to speak productively about political change. Their lives and writing have drawn me in powerfully, breathlessly. They are both similar to and radically different from my own, yet they are continually, and often surprisingly, instructive for delineating links between female genealogy and feminist consciousness. Studying these women's lives in the context of their work forces us to take seriously the complex, unstable, and undeniably concrete experience of sexual particularity. As women, political claims are staked and denied; expectations are met and dashed; life histories unfold; and choices must be made. Significantly, each of the women understands that being a woman is not solely an individual experience but also a collective definition—one that though politically contested and intertwined with class, race, history, culture, and a multitude of other factors must nonetheless be reckoned with.

Culling memoirs, letters, conversations, and literary representations of women both famous and ordinary, Beauvoir's *The Second Sex* offers countless examples of the situation of specific women. She introduces us to women who live only in the eyes of their husbands or lovers; of women who give themselves over to religion; of women who put all their energy into being "good" mothers; of women who spend all their time trying to be beautiful. These examples are of women who conform to the dictates of what she calls the eternal feminine—described as an ideological construction of women as passive, domestic, narcissistic, and unwilling to take on the responsibility of subjectivity—and thus relinquish their potential to be free. She also writes of the ways the eternal feminine even influences women who quite consciously attempt to break out of these restraints and struggle to assume their freedom. She calls these women "independent" and writes that we have much to learn about how being marked as the Other limits the situation of even the most forward-thinking women.

Describing the situation of one of these independent women in a memorable passage, Beauvoir (1989, 501) remarks that "Mme de Staël carried on a pregnancy as readily as a conversation." Yet even Beauvoir, insightful feminist theorist that she was, idealized the strength of individual performative will for one of her feminist mothers. It seems she failed to realize, or at least radically simplified, the ways gender norms might have taken hold within Staël's life. As it turns out, Staël, amazing and independent woman though she was, still had to constantly negotiate the standards of femininity that accompanied her historical epoch and social class. As Staël admitted, there were times she found it exceedingly difficult to live her life as an upper-class intellectual within the body of a woman. In 1803, for example, Staël was judged by Napoleon Bonaparte, who had recently been named First Consul for Life and was heading for the apex of his imperial power, to be such a considerable threat that he had her banished from her beloved Paris. While focusing on her own individual power struggle with Napoleon, Staël's narrative in *Ten Years of Exile* simultaneously reveals the gender structure ruling Napoleonic France. Remarking that she "sensed the tyranny in Bonaparte's character" (Staël 2000, 16), Staël deftly observed that Napoleon would "try to banish women from the earth if he had not needed their children for soldiers" (p. 7). When the chief of gendarmes at Versailles informed Staël that she had a mere twenty-four hours to leave the country, Staël's protests stemmed from the concerns of a woman: "To leave in twenty-four hours was suitable for conscripts but not for a woman and children" (p. 71). When the gendarme compliments her on her writings, Staël glibly retorted, "'You see where being an intelligent woman leads,'" I told him. 'Advise the members of your family against it, if you have the opportunity'" (ibid.).

In another passage, Staël confided her intense fear of isolation and the guilt induced by endangering her friends and taking her children away from the life they had always known. Remaining true to her self-constructed identity as an intellectual woman who was willing to risk all so she could speak out in defense of liberty cost her a great deal. Staël's choices committed her to constant worry about her children. Her five-year-old daughter fell dangerously ill in Frankfurt, and Staël was unable to find a French-speaking doctor; her two older sons risked arrest in appealing to the emperor on her behalf; she was forced to choose between dangerous sea crossings and treacherous land escapes; she subjected her loved ones to her own fate at every turn. She learned that various friends "had been exiled from Paris for maintaining connections" with her (Staël 2000, 115), and lamented that it was "dreadful to be of no use to one's children and to harm one's friends" (p. 118).

Clearly Staël's political commitment to liberty influenced her choices and put her family at risk. In looking at the lives of the women I selected for this book, I found that they were often forced to choose between family or personal happiness and political commitments. Goldman, for example, found that her intense schedule on behalf of the anarchist cause precluded maintaining the kind of prolonged personal intimacy that, as she indicated in her letters, she so strongly desired. In a speech Goldman wrote in 1911, she expressed tribute to the life and work of Wollstonecraft, revealing similar fundamental contradictions in the life of her feminist foremother. Specifically, she focused on the contradictions between the reputation of Wollstonecraft as author of

A Vindication of the Rights of Woman and the private life of the woman who needed, as Goldman contended, "love, unreserved, passionate love" (Goldman 1981, 119).

Wollstonecraft's need for love, as Goldman understood it, is revealed in private letters from Wollstonecraft to her American lover, Gilbert Imlay. Wollstonecraft met Imlay during the heady days of the French Revolution. Believing that with Imlay she might experiment with more democratic forms of domesticity, she fell in love, gave birth to a daughter outside of marriage, and was soon after abandoned by her lover. Her voice in letters to her unreceptive former lover is that of a melancholy, lonely, desperate woman struggling to raise a child by herself in a punitive environment for single mothers. Engulfed with grief at the failure of French Revolutionary goals as well as the failure of her experiment with revolutionary forms of conjugality, Wollstonecraft admitted in one letter that "when I am thus sad, I lament that my little darling, fondly as I doat [sic] on her, is a girl—I am sorry to have a tie to a world that for me is ever sown with thorns" (Wollstonecraft 1979, 273). For some, these aspects of Wollstonecraft's life may seem to conflict with her reputation as author of the most important feminist writing of the eighteenth century, a canonical woman thinker who advocated a vision of women as strong, independent, and potentially rights-bearing individuals. In conjunction with this claim to feminist authority, the fact that Wollstonecraft was sometimes a dependent, needy, and despondent woman did not surprise and, in fact, attracted Goldman.

And it attracts me as well. What particularly strikes me about Wollstonecraft's life when read in the context of her work is how conventional definitions of femininity for a woman of her class limited

her choices. Nancy Hirschmann (2003) has argued that a feminist theory of freedom must take into account not only whether a subject is free to choose but also whether or not she has been able to play a role in constructing the choices in the first place. Though Wollstonecraft understood herself as an unconventional and free woman, when she acted in light of the freedom she claimed for herself she was branded as Staël was by Napoleon: "crazy," "crow," "hussy," and "others still worse" (Goldberger in Staël 2000, ix, xx). This in itself, read as typical misogyny, is hardly surprising. What interests me is how feminist authors such as Staël and Wollstonecraft sought to understand and theorize the relationship between the dictates of conventional femininity—specific to their race and class or as identified for other women in different locations—and what they identified as their own desires as women.

Both Wollstonecraft and Staël gave a great deal of thought to questions addressing how femininity works as a material constraint in women's lives. I explore, for example, how Wollstonecraft and Staël theorized the significance of Marie-Antoinette's struggles with the demands of femininity as dictated by what a woman as queen should signify. Their work on Marie-Antoinette is contrasted with their writings on the Women's March to Versailles of October 1789, the first moment in the Revolution that lower-class women organized as women to make political demands. The contrast between the expectations of femininity for a queen and those of the lower-class market women fascinated both feminist authors; yet, as we will see, they come to different conclusions about the lessons learned for feminists and how to strategically undo or deploy notions of femininity. Extending this argument into their own existential experiments with how femi-

ninity worked in their own lives, I investigate how Wollstonecraft and Staël's understanding of ideals of femininity played a political and emotional role in their lives as women. Along these lines, I read Staël's and Wollstonecraft's travel memoirs framing the meaning of their revolutionary experience in light of their focus on women's needs, including and highlighting their own.

Goldman's life experience made it clear that no true freedom for women could exist without a fundamental revolution in how we understand love and sexuality. She insisted on bringing to light the inequality manifested in our most intimate relationships such as marriage and the nuclear family. Goldman's articulation of the definitions of the demands of femininity vary greatly, however, from those experienced by her black female counterparts within the same historical moment, as witnessed when I compare her work to that of Ida B. Wells on the material constraints of femininity within early twentieth-century American politics. Ida B. Wells was a journalist and co-owner, editor, and publisher of the *Free Speech*, a weekly newspaper in Memphis, Tennessee; in addition to being one of the most well-known black woman suffragists, she initiated the antilynching campaign of the late nineteenth and early twentieth century. Wells's insistent condemnation of lynching brought to light ideals of white womanhood and black manhood inherent to its practice. Wells thus uncovered the myths of black and white masculinity and femininity that were left uninvestigated by Goldman. Alongside my work on Wollstonecraft's and Staël's readings of Marie-Antoinette, I discuss these questions in the work of Goldman and Wells to demonstrate how ideals of femininity always intersect with ideologies of race, class, and sexuality and have material consequences in women's lives. Here, then, I document the demands of femininity as witnessed by Wollstonecraft, Staël, Goldman, and Wells for women of various class and race positions and then in later chapters explore ways women might engage in existential experiments with the feminine within these constraints.

I probe Goldman's life and work more deeply when I read her autobiography and letters alongside her political essays. This critical comparison exposes the existential dilemmas of living within the demands of femininity while trying to undo them in her life and work as a committed feminist anarchist. How Goldman thought about feminist insights as they concerned her own life is gleaned from a study of her letters to her longtime comrade Alexander Berkman. Kathy Ferguson (2002) notes that Goldman's letters to Berkman were often "pamphlet-sized epistles covering a range of topics: friends; acquaintances; their health; former, present and future lovers; the destruction of the revolution in Russia; the place of violence in anarchist struggles; relations between women and men; the vagaries of "the masses"; articles and speeches they helped each other write; finances; books; government harassment of exiles; their own enduring friendship." Goldman left behind literally mountains of letters that reveal her commitment to political life while illuminating the sacrifices such an intense political life required. In one such letter to Berkman written in 1925, Goldman confided:

> We all need love and affection and understanding, and a woman needs a
> damn sight more of that when she grows older. I am sure that is the main
> cause of my misery since I left America. For since then I have had no one,
> or met anyone who gave a fig for what I do and what becomes of me. Of
> course, you dear, I am not speaking of our friendship; that is a thing apart.
> But I mean exactly what you mean, someone intimate, someone personal who
> would take some interest, show affection, and really care. . . . I am consumed by

> longing for love and affection for some human being of my own. I know the
> agony of loneliness and yearning. (Goldman 1975, 128)

How did Goldman stay committed to political change in the face of emotional and financial insecurity, disillusionment, despair, imprisonment, exile, and abandonment by family and lovers? Like Goldman in her work on Wollstonecraft, I am drawn to passages where feminist heroines, in reflecting on their personal choices, express radical self-doubt while simultaneously criticizing the limited choices they were offered. Within the pages of this book, I look to these women's lives to explore their sense of the meanings and attempted redefinitions of the demands of femininity. I do not conflate the demands of femininity with Beauvoir's notion of the eternal feminine, as the demands of femininity are clearly fused with historical expectations about race, class, and sexuality. Yet, one of the surprising things I discover is that none of the feminist thinkers flatly deny any attraction to values and characteristics roughly ascribed to the feminine. All of these feminists find the body and their desires as a woman, however described and understood, to be a defining factor in the choices they make in spite of their disavowal of conforming to the demands of femininity as dictated by men, culture, society, and their moment in history. In this, they would agree with contemporary feminist Judith Butler (1993, 29), who argues that speaking of *women* must occur, but the term should not be reified: "It should stand a chance of being opened up, indeed, of coming to signify in ways that none of us can signify in advance."

In looking to the lives of these women as they struggle with the demands of femininity, I chart their disavowal of these expectations alongside the complex journey each woman takes in making difficult choices about intimacy, children, sexual experimentation, and, in contemporary language, how to balance work, family, and politics. If, for instance, these women chose to forego motherhood, how did they come to this choice, and how did they feel about its implications? Was it a political as much as a personal decision? What about marriage, monogamy, and sexual exploration? The moment of critical reflection on having to follow a path that does not make room for one's own desire, or alternatively, the reflection on society's punishment once one does act freely, illuminates that women have struggles in common stemming from having to negotiate norms of femininity. Awareness of belonging to a community of women might foster political coalitions and make feminist alternatives possible. Could this consciousness of potential community, when articulated within a radical reconsideration of the demands of femininity, guide the feminist project to redefine being a woman alongside other women in the world—this in light of the enormity of differences among women?

Feminist Interlocutors

Sonia Kruks (2001, 152) has argued that "the more we make an effort to learn about women whose lives are radically different from our own, the more do bonds of affinity become possible." Nancy K. Miller (2002, xiii) confesses her passion for reading the stories of other people's lives, acknowledging that she came to see her own life as an "unwitting but irresistible collaboration between other texts and other lives." Miller claims that by learning about the life of someone unlike yourself, you can make connections, that "identification can also mean the desire to rediscover yourself across the body or under the skin of other selves, people who are nothing—seem nothing like yourself" (pp. 11–12). When we turn to the lives of our feminist mothers, women whose lives were in many ways radically unlike our own yet shared similar aspirations and were forced to suffer society's disdain, what do we discover about our own lives?

By attending to and connecting the lives and work of intellectual women—women who think about their desires for freedom and how they work with and against what I have designated as the demands of femininity—we can weave a genealogy that might inspire feminist consciousness. These examples reveal the great difficulty of searching for and claiming authentic freedom in light of the many barriers to it. They also force us to confront internalized desires that lead to the acceptance, and thus perpetuation, of society's conventional definitions and expectations of femininity. Each of the women whose lives and work I have chosen to write about in this book knows that to become a woman in the Beauvoirian sense is to simultaneously participate in a given gender identity as well as to engage in a unique existential project. Conventional definitions of femininity continuously serve to constrain women even when they desire to be free subjects, engaged in their own projects and pursuing their unique and individual desires. As Butler (2004, 3) has put it, "the 'I' that I am finds itself at once constituted by norms and dependent on them but also endeavors to live in ways that maintain a critical and transformative relation to them." Emphasizing the urge toward existential experimenting within the material and psychological demands of femininity extends and deepens the insight that any feminist conception of freedom must take situation and context into account. As feminists, we should be able to make critical comparisons that attend to difference in situation, such as witnessed by the demands of femininity for women in their specific situations. To engage and interrogate these contexts to make such critical comparisons, women must study each other's lives and situations.

When I focus on Beauvoir's life and work, I read her tribute to her dying mother in light of the way feminists have responded to her legacy as our feminist mother. As I have already suggested, I intend to extend and deepen Irigaray's insight that we must reckon with vertical relations between mothers and daughters—including nonbiological relationships—to free ourselves to act politically in feminist horizontal coalitions. Reading Beauvoir's work in light of her life experiences, I ask how reading these women's lives within both maternal and feminist genealogies might help us to articulate a feminist consciousness that acknowledges differences among and between women yet still allows us to speak of women as having certain struggles in common.

Finally, I apply what feminist theorists have taught us about genealogy to probe dilemmas articulated by contemporary feminists within a variety of different locations and contexts. Here I look to radically different accounts of how feminists think about their lives as women, mothers, daughters, as professionals, teachers, and revolutionaries and how these roles often clash in ways that make it painful, but also possible, for them to find fulfillment in creative ways. In reading these accounts I revisit themes earlier identified in this book as they are highlighted in contemporary autobiographies written by feminist intellectuals. These accounts range from a focus on women's role within revolutions and the importance of privileging women's desires through communities of women (e.g., Gioconda Belli's *The Country under My Skin: A Memoir of Love and War* and Azar Nafisi's *Reading Lolita in Tehran*) to the imperative of forging a new feminist consciousness (e.g., Ana Castillo's *Massacre of the Dreamers: Essays on*

Xicanisma) back to the connection to mothers and motherhood (e.g., Steedman's *Landscape for a Good Woman*, Drucilla Cornell's *Legacies of Dignity: Between Women and Generations*, Audre Lorde's *Zami: A New Spelling of My Name*, and Uma Narayan's *Dislocating Cultures: Identities, Traditions, and Third-World Feminism*).

Steedman (1986), for example, tells the story of her mother's life and death, which as a working-class life differed radically from that of Beauvoir's mother, to capture its particularity and to tell her unique story. Having come of age in a home full of her mother's "terrible tiredness and terrible resentment" (p. 39), Steedman looks back on her mother's life as a counterpoint to Beauvoir's story of her mother's death. But Steedman also extends beyond this singular story to explore how desire—in this case her mother's desire for material comfort—shaped her own and her daughter's consciousness and the circumstances of their lives: "The faces of the women in the queues are the faces of unfulfilled desire; if we look, there are many women driven mad in this way, as my mother was. This is a sad and secret story, but it isn't just hers alone" (p. 22). It is not just hers alone. What effect does the unfulfilled desire of the mother have on the daughter's life? Writing about her life growing up in a middle-class home in Bombay, India, documenting why and how she became a feminist, Narayan (1997, 6–7) remembers the gender dynamics of her family:

> I remember minding particularly that the injunction to be silent came from my mother, who told me so early, because she had no one else to tell, about her sufferings in her conjugal home. I remember my mother's anger and grief at my father's resort to a silencing "neutrality" that refused to "interfere" in the domestic tyrannies that his mother inflicted on my mother. The same mother who complained about her silencing enjoined me to silence, doing what she had to do, since my failures to conform would translate as

her failures to rear me well.

Yet the silencing of her mother taught Narayan a different lesson. Narayan's mother complained that her daughter had not grown up to be a "good Indian woman," and Narayan responded—not directly to her mother but later in print—"But mother, you were not entirely silent. You laid it all on me. My earliest memory (you were the one who dated it after I described it to you, and were amazed that I remember it) is of seeing you cry. I heard all your stories of misery. The shape your 'silence' took is in part what has incited me to speech" (p. 7).

Like Beauvoir and Narayan, Steedman was attempting to understand the complexities of her mother's unfulfilled desire so that she could escape that destiny. She wanted, most of all, not to become her mother, not to replay the mistakes and unfulfilled longings, not to live that "straitened, unsatisfying life"—all this, though, without condemning her mother's desire. On the contrary, Steedman infused her mother's desire with political meaning. What she wanted was "a full skirt that took twenty yards of cloth, a half-timbered cottage in the country, the prince who did not come" (Steedman 1986, 47). Even though she had two daughters, Steedman's mother did not wish for children for their own sake. Her rejection of the desire for children points toward a political truth, one that Steedman argues is left unrecognized by the feminist literature: "It is to marginal and secret stories that we have to look for any disturbance of the huge and bland assumption that the wish for a child largely structures femininity; and that modern feminism sees the reproduction of the wish as a *problem* makes it no less of an assumption that the wish is consistently present in all women, in all places and times" (p. 4).

The daughter, Steedman (1986, 7), consciously rejects motherhood to become, as she put it, a woman who by refusing to mother refused "to reproduce themselves or the circumstances of their exile." As Giddings (1984, 45) noted of black women under slavery, "the most dramatic and least known act of resistance was the refusal of slave women to perform their most essential role, producing baby slaves, for which they were rewarded." And yet, Steedman, like the slave women, in refusing maternity still reckoned with the meaning of motherhood, the choice to mother or not, and her role as daughter. As Miller (1997, 1002) reminds us, "Mother is the intractable (beloved, admired, or feared) Other through whom we come to understand ourselves not just as women but as members of this sex that we've learned—again from Irigaray—is not one."

From Nicaragua, celebrated poet and author Giaconda Belli (2002, 105) also struggles with expectations, the demands, and the feminine presence of the mother as this excerpt recounts.

> My mother was a petite, delicate, and difficult woman. She denied herself the intensity of her feelings but, in hard times, she always rose to the occasion, revealing herself as the extraordinary woman she was. Sometimes I see so many similarities between her and me. We both wanted to push the limits, and I think she resented me for being the one to dare. She had chosen obligation. And I had chosen my dreams. The ebb and flow of her love wavered between pushing me away or drawing me close. She wanted me to keep afloat until I reached port, nurtured by the primeval waters of her womb, but I knew that her waters would engulf me. I needed to swim far away. I wanted to be another ocean. I don't think she ever understood, she never knew what to make of me.

And across cultures again, this time from Iran, literature professor and author Azar Nafisi (2003) reflects on a similar situation. The struggles enacted between and across obligations, generations, and within the changing definitions of tradition as defined through colonial struggle is illuminated in Nafisi's memoir. She wrote specifically about the struggle with her mother's idea of being a "lady" in an "Islamic country."

> My mother would go crazy each time she saw the paintings leaning against the wall and the vases of flowers on the floor and the curtainless windows, which I refused to dress until I was finally reminded this was an Islamic country and windows needed to be dressed. I don't know if you really belonged to me, she would lament. Didn't I raise you to be orderly and organized? Her tone was serious, but she had repeated the same complaint for so many years that by now it was almost a tender ritual. Azi—that was my nickname—Azi, she would say, you are a grown-up lady now; act like one. Yet there was something in her tone that kept me young and fragile and obstinate, and still, when in memory I hear her voice, I know I never lived up to her expectations. I never did become the lady she tried to will me into being. (p. 7)

Does examining the mother's life help the daughter become a feminist? This is a question I explore throughout. I argue that a feminist consciousness of the situations of our mothers is crucial for coalition. In noting the various definitions of conventional femininity for black and white women, Giddings (1984, 54) documented the way the cult of true womanhood left a bitter legacy for both, noting finally that "if the two [black and white women] had been able to work together to challenge their respective images, there is no telling what could have happened."

How does a woman face up as truthfully as she can to the circumstances and unfulfilled desires of the mother's life? The stories of the lives of feminists are incomplete if we look only to professional and political achievement, of steady movement toward increasing freedom. We also must consider anxiety, pain, longing, frustration, demands unmet, expectations dashed, and the damning, judgmental constraints of conventional femininity that always lie in wait for each feminist trying to create new meanings for being a woman.

These are more than each woman's personal issues; the dilemmas experienced are the result of the gender dynamics and the material conditions of femininity within each woman's historical and political moment. Linking our knowledge of the unfulfilled desires of the mothers who raised us with similar struggles faced by feminist thinkers and writers joins us in a genealogical community of women. We must take the step of making political connections to other women to achieve feminist solidarity. As Narayan (1997, 11) powerfully reminds us:

> An awareness of the gender dynamics within one's family and one's "culture," even a critical awareness, does not suffice to make women feminists. Women may be aware of such dynamics but may consider them to be *personal* problems to be dealt with personally, without seeing them as a *systematic* part of the ways in which their family, their "culture," and changing material and social conditions script gender roles and women's lives, or without feeling that they must contest them in more formal, public, and political ways. It takes *political connections* to other women and their experiences, political analyses of women's problems, and attempts to construct political solutions for them, to make women into feminists in any full-blooded sense, as the history of women's movements in various parts of the world shows us.

Beauvoir convincingly argued that her own achievements as an individual woman—as a philosopher, a writer, a public figure—were not in any way sufficient to signal a change for ordinary women. Though she, as an individual, achieved great prominence and independence, the situation of the great majority of women remained unchanged. By exploring feminist genealogies, I intentionally link the lives of intellectual and independent women with women who do not have the same opportunities due to their situations. Beauvoir argued repeatedly that liberation must be a collective project and that women must achieve economic independence to struggle toward psychological forms of freedom. How might the lives of intellectual women, and their quest for freedom, shed light on feminist strategies to achieve the ultimate goal of eliminating the need for a feminist movement?

Throughout this book I emphasize that consciousness of sexual difference—understood as claiming placement in a community of women while rejecting the demands of conventional femininity—is key to forging a feminist movement. This is clearly not an uncontroversial statement given feminist fears of being labeled a "gender essentialist." If one identifies as a woman, for example, does it indicate an acceptance of conventional definitions that come with such identification? Moreover, and more dangerously perhaps, does one's acknowledgment of being a woman trump or deny other aspects of one's identity? I argue within this book that it does not. In fact, I claim that it is necessary to identify as women, within female and feminist genealogies, to move feminism forward. This does not imply complete understanding or identification with all the experiences of all women, nor can it be reduced to simple essentialism. Invoking a community of women, I simultaneously interrogate how this community might be constituted. Within this book, I hope to articulate a framework for addressing experiences of difference among women without effacing the category. Because despite claims from many quarters that we live in a "post-feminist" society, becoming and being a woman has distinct consequences for our lived experiences in the world.

The different chapters in this book explore how sexual difference acquires meaning in relation to the needs, demands, limitations, and imaginative possibilities of living as a woman, with the consciousness of feminism, in different historical eras. To make other women our privileged interlocutors—to attempt to sympathize with the experiences of women struggling toward freedom—is to privilege the accounts of women, and in this case our feminist mothers and contemporaries, to discover, to engage, and to interrogate our own struggles toward freedom.

2. Women's Situation, I

The Material Constraints of Femininity

By way of introduction to the second part of *The Second Sex*, where Simone de Beauvoir (1989, 267) described women's lives as they live them—what she calls women's lived reality—she contended, "One is not born, but rather becomes, a woman." I take this venerated phrase as my motif for the next two chapters and, indeed, as a way to frame this book. Each of the feminist thinkers whose lives and work I present here engages in what I call existential experiments with the feminine within the material constraints of femininity. Though feminists, they each had to grapple with the implications and complications of becoming and being women. Even as feminists, they were seen and objectified as possessing certain group traits (called the eternal feminine by Beauvoir) at moments when they hoped to create their lives as free subjects. Despite the fact that they deliberately rejected official norms of femininity, these feminists often found themselves trapped within structures and situations that explicitly limited their actions and are often reflected in interpretations of their work. Moreover, their material circumstances and, more surprisingly perhaps, their subjective experience of the world, remained deeply influenced by the demands and standards of femininity. Thus, I chronicle and interpret what each feminist theorist was compelled to explore: the significance of criticizing the constraints of femininity while simultaneously having to act within them.

Struggling for Freedom within Situation

To set the context for these issues, I clarify what Beauvoir means by the concepts of freedom and situation to explain the existentialist approach and why I employ it here. Beauvoir (1989, xxxiv) wrote *The Second Sex* from the perspective of what she called "existentialist ethics." Within this approach, freedom is prized as the highest good, defined as "a continual reaching out toward other liberties" into "an indefinitely open future" (pp. xxxiv, xxxv). To authentically claim one's freedom is to take risks, to make a mark on the world, to act, to transcend. But for Beauvoir, to assume authentic freedom is not to act selfishly. To act freely in accordance with existentialist ethics one must always remain cognizant of the effect of one's actions on others in the world. Hence, freedom is political as well as collective. This distinguishes Beauvoir's existential approach from that of liberals, wherein freedom is singular, autonomous, selfish, and absolutely individual.

Moreover, Beauvoir's view of freedom cannot be conflated with that of her famous existentialist partner, Jean Paul Sartre. Distinguishing her view of freedom from Sartre's, Beauvoir (1989) offers an account of the subject and her freedom as situated and embodied. The subject is always already within situation as well as always within a body. The subject's relationship to the world is constituted by the materiality of her body such as sexuality, race or ethnicity, enabledness, age, physical prowess, and so forth. Moreover, the body itself is "not a thing" but rather a "situation" (p. 34). Depending on the factors previously mentioned, the body "is the instrument of our grasp upon the world, a limiting factor for our projects" (ibid.). Clearly, freedom for the subject is never unlimited, never a phenomenon of consciousness alone. Rather, freedom is constituted within bodily, national, class, historical, and cultural situations. Being a woman is but one factor with which the individual woman must contend. As Toril Moi (1999, 68) helpfully describes, "if I have to negotiate the world in a crippled body or sick body I am not going to have the same experience of the world or of myself as if I had a healthy or particularly athletic body…nor will the world react to me in the way it would if I had a different body." How our bodies are perceived in the world becomes one of the material circumstances that significantly contribute to our unique experience as individuals.

In Beauvoir's thinking, one's material situation, as well as the reaction to and perception of this material situation, constitutes the subject's relationship to her world. Moi (1999, 60) articulates that "for Beauvoir, the body perceived as a situation is deeply related to the individual woman's (or man's) subjectivity." Beauvoir was able to theorize a subject who is both self-constituting as well as constituted by structures not of her making. The individual subject experiences desires and may be capable of achieving freedom, but only within a body and a world not necessarily of her choosing. This is a concept of freedom in restraint, of choice and of consciousness as intimately linked to the situation in which one finds oneself at any given moment in time.

Significantly, Beauvoir (1989, xxvii) characterizes the struggle to achieve freedom as extremely difficult for each human subject. As she put it, "along with the ethical urge of each individual to affirm his subjective existence, there is also the temptation to forego liberty and become a thing." Beauvoir further demonstrated that foregoing the quest for liberty is even more tempting for women than for men. She theorizes that women have more difficulty embracing freedom due to the influence of the eternal feminine wherein woman is characterized as passive, resigned, patient, dependent, inferior, and immanent. My theorization of the demands of femininity extends Beauvoir's theory of the eternal feminine in that I show how standards of femininity vary for women in terms of race, class, and historical and cultural location. Like the eternal feminine, though, the demands of femininity are continually present in all women's lives. They play a central role in defining women's expectations and shaping women's desires.

Though Beauvoir (1989) recognized constraints on freedom, she consistently valued its exercise. And while we always experience freedom in relationship to others, rather than singularly and alone, situations that unduly limit our freedom are said to be problematic: "Every time transcendence falls back into immanence, stagnation, there is a degradation of existence into the *en-soi*—the brutish life of subjection to given conditions—and of liberty into constraint and contingence. This downfall represents a moral fault if the subject consents to it; if it is inflicted upon him, it spells frustration and oppression. In both cases it is an absolute evil" (p. xxxv). Women's situation, characterized by an inability to exercise—and maybe even an inability to desire—freedom, accounts for women's passivity, dependence, obedience, powerlessness, bitterness, and rage. Though many of Beauvoir's remarks on women's character may seem at first glance to caricaturize women, Beauvoir constantly and consistently argued that these aspects of women's personalities are to be understood as arising from particular situations.[1] Often, for example, women are complicit in desiring their subordination. Sometimes women even claim that they are happy in embracing the role that femininity has set for their particular location. Beauvoir (1989) warns us, however, that labeling as happy the women who appears to choose her immanence, or embrace her Otherness, is a mistake. She insists that "there is no possibility of measuring the happiness of others, and it is always easy to describe as happy the situation in which one wishes to place them" (p. xxxiv). As Beauvoir articulated, "what peculiarly signalizes the situation of woman is that she—a free and autonomous being like all human creatures—nevertheless finds herself living in a world where men compel her to assume the status of the Other" (ibid.).

Beauvoir argued that women throughout history "have always been subordinated to men" (1989, xxiv). As human beings, women possess the potential to act in accordance with authentic freedom, yet since their situations are "profoundly different," men "have many more opportunities to exercise [their] freedom in the world" (p. 627). Thus, most often it is women who find themselves within situations that deny them the opportunity to seek freedom. Since men "have always kept in their hands all concrete powers" (p. 139), "all comparisons are idle which purport to show that woman is superior, inferior, or equal to man, for their situations are profoundly different" (p. 627). In her reading of women's lives, Beauvoir showed that women break out of these confines all the time, but they always must struggle against them, and this struggle for women is much more difficult than that for men.

Moi (1999, 8) clarifies that "any given woman will transcend the category of femininity, however it is defined." Thus, though categorized by gender, women, like men, are singular individuals, always embedded in situation. Situation and one's response to it are the key factors for Beauvoir. Therefore, what Beauvoir designated as situation is a complex combination between subjective response and objective circumstance, and it is not gender construction alone that influences the character of men and women. Beauvoir (1989, 627) concluded that it is "as absurd, then, to speak of 'woman' in general as of the 'eternal' man."

Situation is thus a complex dialectic involving both material circumstances and one's response to them. Neither biology nor social and cultural norms adequately account for the differences between men and women and the way each is perceived and treated in the world. Neither alone determines the creation of sexually different beings in the world, for it is the significance of sexual difference as experienced both materially and subjectively that accounts for one's lived reality. Indeed, it is the lived reality of human beings that reveals the significance of sexual differences. There are embodied, sexually different human beings in the world who are called monsters when perceived as acting or being outside the norm.

The thinkers I study within this book all seek to envision and live new ways of being women while struggling with the demands of femininity as they understand and experience them. I briefly explore the conditions of women's situation under the material demands of femininity as Mary Wollstonecraft and Germaine de Staël defined it in the early stages of the French Revolution and then as Emma Goldman and Ida B. Wells theorized it in early twentieth-century

America within the struggle to remove obstacles to black suffrage and achieve women's suffrage. Whereas later chapters focus on the struggles of individual feminist intellectuals to move beyond the ways they are defined—materially and psychologically—by femininity, this chapter demonstrates how the ideological construction of femininity locates women of various classes and races within particular social categories.

I isolate the October 1789 Women's March to Versailles and the August 1793 Trial of Marie-Antoinette to study here alongside Goldman's and Wells's political intervention in the struggle for women's suffrage in the United States. In each of these historical moments, the status of femininity and women's role in politics are central. The women's march was the first time in the Revolution that women came together as a group to act politically and to make demands of their sovereigns. One of these sovereigns, Marie-Antoinette, herself was slandered and then executed for stepping outside the role of proper femininity. Likewise, the cult of true womanhood dominates the ideal of proper femininity in late nineteenth- and early twentieth-century American politics precisely at the moment when both black and white women were demanding that their political voices be heard. The writings of Wollstonecraft, Staël, Goldman, and Wells on how the idea of femininity was manipulated show their own awareness of the material conditions of femininity—that is, how the idea places women in particular locations—while also revealing the ways these feminists attempted to make political interventions on behalf of women as a group.

The Queen and Market Women: Mary Wollstonecraft and Germaine de Staël

I shall therefore only speak of that verdict, analyzing the political, in telling what I have seen, what I know of the queen, and in depicting the hideous circumstances which have led to her condemnation.

Germaine de Staël, *Reflections*
on the Trial of the Queen, by a Woman, August 1793

Staël's essay in defense of Marie-Antoinette at the time of her trial was initially published anonymously as authored only by a woman. That Staël identified herself as a woman is significant. The Revolutionary Criminal Tribunal, consisting of a male jury and nine male judges, ultimately decided Marie-Antoinette's fate, yet the lower-class women of Paris were among her most notorious and vicious enemies. Indeed, the first time that women organized politically as a group of women was to march to Versailles in October 1789 to demand that the royal couple guarantee bread to the people and approve the Declaration of the Rights of Man and of the Citizen. The direct confrontation between the Queen of France and the mostly lower-class Parisian women who marched to Versailles to capture the queen serves as a political moment open to a variety of readings.

In the bill of indictment against Marie-Antoinette at her trial, she was accused of squandering public monies, of siphoning money to Austria, and, most outrageously, of engaging in incest with her son. A host of contemporary feminist scholars have studied the ways Marie-Antoinette's status as queen symbolized, for revolutionaries, the feminization and corruption of the Old Regime. Propaganda at the time painted Marie-Antoinette as woman, foreigner, prostitute, adulteress, and coquette. And indeed, the trial and execution of the queen in August 1793 marked the moment after which all possibilities for women's formal participation in politics were closed off.

Notice the interpretive and political perils of these historical events for writers who sought to advance women's potential role in the New Republic. Marie-Antoinette, the female victim said to symbolize the feminine excess of the aristocracy, is attacked by lower-class market women testing and enacting their newly found political power. How was the feminist writer to understand the potential role of women in politics and notions of the feminine when faced with such contradictory behavior of women and diverse meaning attached to the feminine?[2] To attempt to analyze the role of women in these events, one becomes increasingly drawn into an eighteenth-century discursive dynamic of the politics of sense and sensibility. Simply put, sensibility was identified with female virtues of sympathetic feeling, empathetic behavior, and romanticism; sense was associated with masculine rational discourse as exemplified in Enlightenment philosophy. Negotiating the gendered politics of sense and sensibility proved to be a significant challenge for women who wished to see gender inequality alleviated. To continue to associate women and to define the feminine self through the lens of sensibility was to run the risk of identifying women with the very qualities that had been said to justify their exclusion from politics in the first place. To turn the tables and to claim that women could indeed be associated with sense just as well as men was to risk reifying a masculine model of political discourse rendering sexual difference incompatible with democratic politics.

Wollstonecraft and Staël boldly entered into this debate. Wollstonecraft, a writer of the middle classes who wrote to earn her keep, firmly forged her allegiance with the common people in analyzing the conditions of the majority, claiming that women faced the most wretched circumstances of all. And despite the increasing radicalization of the Revolution, until her death in 1797 Wollstonecraft remained committed to the view of the "French Revolution [as] part of the human destiny for improvement" and sought to secure the rights of her sex through democratic politics (Sapiro 1996, 39).

In contrast, Staël, daughter of Jacques Necker, finance minister on the eve of the Revolution, and Suzanne Necker, Parisian salonnière, was an aristocrat by birth and initially sought to prepare herself to preside over a salon and "exert an influence in the manner appropriate to women of the aristocracy" (Fraisse 1994, 104). Initially loyal to the idea of an enlightened constitutional monarchy, Staël became a committed republican. Swept up into the center of revolutionary events by her father's position, Staël remained fascinated by politics—and especially the role of women—throughout her life and put these concerns at the forefront of her work. Though the lives of women were central to almost everything Staël wrote, she was most interested in the lives of exceptional women and never explicitly made the case for politically empowering every woman. After the fall of the monarchy, Staël took refuge in Switzerland, returned to France in 1795, eventually became a forceful opponent of Napoleon Bonaparte, and was exiled in 1803. Her three-volume treatise, *Considerations on the Principal Events of the French Revolution*, was left unfinished in 1817 upon her death and was published one year later.

Throughout the revolutionary period interpretations of femininity, what it meant to be a woman, and what that might signify politically and socially were continually in flux. The changing roles of women throughout the various stages of the Revolution have been studied extensively. Dena Goodman (1994) noted that the "querelle des femmes," or woman question, raged throughout the seventeenth and eighteenth centuries. In the Old Regime, upper-class women like Staël's mother presided over salons where ideas were freely exchanged and opinions were circulated. Goodman notes that the salonnière's role "as civilizer was the historical key to the realization of sociability and civilization" (p. 5). These salons played a central role in the Old Regime's reputation as a feminized space. As salonnières rarely published anything, their speech was not seen as dangerous or threatening. These women typified notions of female beauty, sociability, and charm central to the aristocratic definitions of the female gender as rooted in sensibility. Goodman argued that the salonnière's difference as a woman from the men she governed and her position, therefore, outside their discourse shored her legitimacy in the Old Regime.

The work of Jean-Jacques Rousseau, however, set in motion changing conceptions of the roles of women. In his *Politics and the Arts: Letter to M. D'Alembert on the Theatre*, Rousseau (1960, 101) warned against the feminizing effects Old Regime salons have on the men who frequent them. He likened salons to "voluntary prisons" for "harem[s] of men more womanish" than the women who reside over them. Urging women to return to home and hearth, Rousseau claimed that only when women embrace their roles as mothers and wives can men become excellent citizens. He wrote, "Let mothers deign to nurse their children, morals will reform themselves, nature's sentiments will be awakened in every heart, the state will be repeopled. This first point, this point alone, will bring everything back together" (Rousseau 1979, 46).

Rousseau worried that even within the cloistered space of the salon, the delicate balance between men and women, their gender boundaries, and accompanying social duties were beginning to erode. As the Revolution ushered in changing definitions of public and private, women were ideologically situated vis-à-vis each domain. Considered charming in private, the influence of women's speech in public was newly being rendered as a threat to public order.[3]

Thus, the dominant model of femininity became that of the domestic woman, conjuring images of warmth, sensitivity, selflessness, and timidity. The many women who deviated from this norm were classed into a variety of negative stereotypes. Dominique Godineau (1998, xvii–xix) discussed depictions of lower-class female militants as *tricoteuses,* or knitters, so called because they would knit while following debates in the assembly. The *tricoteuse* was seen as a dangerous woman, daring to cross the threshold between home and politics, private and public, ready to ignite violence with her fetish, the needle.

While some upper-class women embraced Rousseau's rhetoric of feminine sensibility, which was exemplified by the call for women to breastfeed their children, others, like the *tricoteuse*, demanded inclusion in shaping changing political realities. The complexity of women's lives and their involvement in the Revolution cannot be captured by the static definitions of femininity available at the moment. Mary Jacobus (1995, 217) noted, for instance, that the "Society of Revolutionary Republican Women defined themselves from the start in terms of their refusal to remain in the 'confined sphere of their households.'" Feminist historians of the French Revolution have reminded us that women were political actors throughout the process and clearly did not always speak in a unified voice. Especially between 1789 and 1793, women were a visible presence in political clubs, popular societies, festivals, and demonstrations. Women participated actively in the reorganization of the municipal government in Paris and in demands for a constitutional monarchy, the fall of the monarchy, and the establishment of the republic. Joan Landes (1995) explained that women did not always speak from concerns for their families and sustenance. Godineau (1998) elaborated that though issues of subsistence often initiated the formation of female crowds, the more militant of these women clearly saw their engagement in revolutionary action as expressive of their wish to participate in political life more generally. Women's marches for bread, sugar, and other essentials were part of the process of women's politicization, and these demands were part of the quest for "political goals such as citizen rights" (Landes 1995, 207). Darline Gay Levy and Harriet B. Applewhite (1992, 89) studied instances of women's militant citizenship linked to the use of force to find that up through summer 1792, "an emerging concept and practice of female citizenship was dissolving distinctions between active/passive citizens, male/female citizens, and public/private roles." Moreover, the great variety of instances of women's political action points to a plurality of perspectives expressed by women. Of the Women's March to Versailles, Madelyn Gutwirth (1992, 239) remarks that though it is commonly thought that the women marched to demand bread, the women's hunger was but "a mere metaphor for the variety and ramifications of their displeasure." They marched to Versailles to demand not only bread but also arms and the return of the sovereigns to Paris.

What is particularly interesting about Wollstonecraft's analysis of the Women's March and the Queen's trial is that she found gender excess—feminine weakness and male vice, but male vice as enacted by women—responsible for the explosive situation brought on during the October Days. She desired, as an enlightened alternative, that we respond to the troubles of the weak regardless of their gender. David

Bromwich (1995, 620) points out that according to Wollstonecraft, "[W]e must feel the evil of wicked acts strongly, sympathetically, with the weight of a judging conscience that is neither masculine nor feminine, and on behalf of the weak who are bound neither to be nor to resemble women." As a response, then, to the demands of femininity on both classes of women, Wollstonecraft hoped for an alternative beyond gender. The distinction of sex, according to Wollstonecraft, should not have salience in matters of individuality. All human creatures have sufficient strength of mind to pursue her definition of virtue, which includes the development of independence in the body, mind, and heart. In her *Vindication of the Rights of Woman*, Wollstonecraft (1988, 9) argued, against Rousseau, that virtue should result from the exercise of reason rather than from refining "slavish dependence, weak delicacy of mind, exquisite sensibility, and sweet docility of manners," qualities currently considered virtuous for the weaker vessel.

According to Wollstonecraft's *Vindication of the Rights of Woman*, the problem with the queen was that she was taught to be a woman, the ultimate model of femininity. Wollstonecraft desired that women eschew ideals of feminine beauty. She realized that Edmund Burke's sympathy for beauty in distress, for example, forces women into subservient roles, dependent on men. As Wollstonecraft (1988, 9) wrote, "I wish to persuade women to endeavor to acquire strength, both of mind and body, and to convince them that the soft phrases, susceptibility of heart, delicacy of sentiment, and refinement of taste are almost synonymous with epithets of weakness, and that those beings who are only the objects of pity and that kind of love, which has been termed its sister, will soon become objects of contempt."

Wollstonecraft (1989a, 72–74) depicted Marie-Antoinette as essentially untrustworthy: She "smiled but to deceive"; she was a "profound dissembler"; "when her family and favorites stood on the brink of ruin, her little portion of mind was employed only to preserve herself from danger." Wollstonecraft argues, moreover, that as a person Marie-Antoinette did not display any "vigor of mind," her "lovely face...hid the want of intelligence," her conversation was "insipid," and she was a "complete actress" adept in "all the arts of coquetry that debauch the mind, whilst they render the person alluring" (pp. 72–74). Furthermore, Wollstonecraft implied that Marie-Antoinette was actually guilty of many of the crimes of which the French people accused her at the time of her trial. She wasted money on frivolities (she was "firmly attached to the aggrandizement of her house"), she sent money abroad to her family in Austria ("she never omitted sending immense sums to her brother, on every occasion"), and she had enormous influence (an "unbounded sway") over the king (pp. 73–74).

Wollstonecraft's (1989a) discourse is reminiscent of the kind of rhetoric that, according to contemporary feminist scholars, served to scapegoat Marie-Antoinette as a bad mother, a dissimulator, an enemy of the people, and the prime example of disorderly femininity. Yet, unlike the propagandists who sought only to slander Marie-Antoinette, Wollstonecraft blamed the queen's shortcomings—which she summed up as lack of virtue—on a lack of education. But she had no kinder words for the common women and ultimately defended the queen in light of what she saw as the excessive violence of the marchers. These women, according to Wollstonecraft, had abandoned the traditional virtues of femininity only to adopt the vices of masculinity. Wollstonecraft branded the marchers as masculine ruffians. She called the group "the lowest refuse of the streets," mostly "market women" who had "thrown off the virtues of one sex without having power to assume more than the vices of the other" (pp. 196–97). She noted that "such a rabble has seldom been gathered together," that they acted "like a gang of thieves," and that their movement "was not the effect of public spirit" (pp. 197–98). She elaborated, "The laws had been trampled on by a gang of banditti the most desperate—The altar of humanity had been profaned—The dignity of freedom had been tarnished—The sanctuary of repose, the asylum of care and fatigue, the chaste temple of a women, I consider the queen only as one…was violated with murderous fury" (p. 209).

The French Revolution inspired in Wollstonecraft the hope that enlightenment and reason would illuminate political life and that virtue would serve as the goal. Women and men, nobles and common-ers, could conceivably participate in this process equally as citizens. In Wollstonecraft's mind, what was necessary for this to occur was a commitment to social change that would produce conditions of equality and a system of education that would guide the populace to embody these qualities.

Thus, Wollstonecraft made her respect for enlightenment, reason, and virtue primary while warning of the danger of assigning particu-lar virtues to each sex. It was the exaggerated femininity of the queen's behavior and the exaggerated masculinity of the marchers' behavior that Wollstonecraft found to be most insidious. Disassociating gender traits from particular bodies, Wollstonecraft hoped to replace the notion of gendered virtue with a singular standard of enlightenment virtue. Part and parcel of this project was the attack on the sensibility standard as connected to women's mental and physical debility. Her vision of egalitarian feminism would release us from both gender and class norms and expectations. But is this at the risk of making sexual difference incompatible with democratic politics?

In Staël's vision, we see an alternative interpretation of these events and the role that the idea of femininity plays within them. She clearly recognized the constraints of the category of femininity on both the queen and the market women, yet she strategically embraced these characteristics of the feminine to forge women's coalition across class boundaries. In direct opposition to Wollstonecraft, Staël invoked traditional notions of femininity as associated with sensibility, suffering, generosity, and pity to attempt to forge a strategic alliance among women of all classes. Staël's rhetorical stance whereby she valorized the attributes of a stereotyped femininity to call for women's inclusion in revolutionary politics was rooted in her burgeoning awareness that to be a woman was increasingly becoming a political fact—an attribute to which revolutionaries attached an overwhelming significance. For Staël, this becomes most clear when looking at the significance that Marie-Antoinette took on as a public and visible woman and in the way women's revolutionary activity and women's desire to participate in revolutionary politics were viewed.

Staël (1818a, 340) praised the group of "women and children, armed with pikes and scythes" whose "political rage became appeased" on "seeing the queen as a mother" (p. 343). When the crowd saw the queen, "her hair disheveled, her countenance pale, but dignified" (ibid.) standing alongside her two children, "those, who that very night had perhaps wished to assassinate her extolled her name to the skies" (ibid.). Staël had the remarkable foresight to realize that Marie-Antoinette was not simply a fallen queen. Her image was being manipulated to represent a too-powerful and too-political woman. Staël worried that if women failed to defend the queen, the most prominent and visible woman in France, women's future in the Revolution might be forever compromised. As Lynn Hunt (1991, 123) reminded us, Marie-Antoinette was accused of crimes mostly on account of her sex: "Promiscuity, incest, poisoning of the heir to the throne, plots to replace the heir with a pliable substitute—all of these charges reflect a fundamental anxiety about queenship as the most extreme form of women invading the public sphere." Anne Mini (1995, 234) added that the essence of Staël's defense of the queen hinges on an account of how Marie-Antoinette's roles as woman suddenly "crashed into one another—roles over which the young queen had even less control than most women." Mini elaborated that on Staël's criteria, condemned as a woman, Marie-Antoinette was simply seen as "asking for it":

> She was famous—and since, society's logic runs, no virtuous woman attracts public attention, she must necessarily have been lacking in virtue. She was wealthy—and since no woman can deserve wealth on her own behalf, she must have stolen it from the French people, using her feminine wiles to distract attention from her avarice....She was the king's wife—and therefore must have used her feminine wiles to blandish him into bad policies, since as a woman, she could not possess the reason to favor good ones....She was the daughter of Maria-Theresa—and thus must have been a traitoress to France. (p. 243)

Thus, Marie-Antoinette's worst crime was to be a highly visible woman. Mini reminds us of something Wollstonecraft had pointed out quite forcefully: Marie-Antoinette did not step out of the prescribed social roles for women. Yet her adherence to those social roles, especially when they crashed into one another, was no guarantee that she would not be slandered. To many women who supported

the Revolution, hatred of Marie-Antoinette came to symbolize their loyalty to the Revolution. Though the queen adhered to a feminine role, in the context of revolutionary politics, many women came to hate the queen for having escaped the traditional female vices: ignorance, poverty, sexual bondage, slavery to their reproductive lives, and unfreedom to act (Gutwirth 1992, 242–43). In Hunt's (1991, 123) analysis, "the queen, then, was the emblem (and sacrificial victim) of the feared disintegration of gender boundaries that accompanied the Revolution."

This paradoxical political situation sheds light on Staël's strategy of invoking a stereotyped notion of the female self. Recall that Staël's political strategy was born in a crucial moment. Staël felt quite certain that manipulation of the image of the queen as the most visible political woman would have dire political consequences for women as a whole in terms of revolutionary politics. Her appeal in the face of this danger, and at the moment of Marie-Antoinette's trial, sought to forge a female community across class and political boundaries by strategically suggesting that the hearts of all women would recognize the queen's plight. Though the women marchers and the queen were class enemies, they were acting in a political moment when the category of woman was being manipulated within revolutionary rhetoric. In both historical as well as contemporary terms, the salient question becomes: When is it possible and politically strategic to invoke categories of identity that have heretofore served as disciplinary or exclusionary? Though marks of identity are oppressive, they are also constitutive of a person's very existence. At the moment of the Women's March, the class oppression of the Old Regime, the queen's status as foreigner and

as woman, and French women's revolutionary role were simultaneously in flux.

Staël was clearly aware that it is precisely because of the inability to
posit a strict feminine subjectivity that the category of woman is open
to both overt and covert forms of political manipulation. In champi-
oning the emotive and the performative as against the rational and
the transparent, Staël willingly engaged in the political acts by which
women must claim political space and action despite the risks inherent
in any such political strategy. Moreover, despite—or maybe because
of—our inability to transparently read the intentions of the marchers
and to understand their own sense of conceptions of womanhood and
feminine subjectivity, it is imperative to theorize how best women can
act in the name of women without attributing a regulatory and disciplinary categorical status to the concept of woman.

Turning the tables on stereotyped notions of identity, however,
can be an exclusionary and very dangerous political move. Though I
am interested in exploring how women may be able to act as women
together in coalition, most often when gender is isolated as a defining
characteristic, it serves to recognize only one version of the material
constraints of femininity for one particular group of women. In the
next section of this chapter, I explore the way the ideal of the cult of
true womanhood as a standard for white middle-class women operated within early twentieth-century American politics to regulate
white women's lives simultaneously and in conjunction with ideals
of black femininity and black masculinity. Goldman and Wells both
fought against these regulatory categories but, like Wollstonecraft and
Staël, failed to notice ways they could work together to undo specific

categories of femininity—always bound with race and class—across racial and class boundaries.

The Cult of True Womanhood and the Antilynching Campaign: Emma Goldman and Ida B. Wells

Much like Wollstonecraft and Staël, Goldman and Wells were feminist contemporaries who never worked together. Also much like Wollstonecraft and Staël, each woman sought to uncover and demystify myths of femininity and true womanhood. Writing within the political context of late nineteenth- and early twentieth-century American society, Wells and Goldman, both outspoken advocates of free speech, were caught up in the battle over the meanings attached to femininity at a time when black men had been granted, but were, by a variety of means, being denied suffrage,[4] and when black and white women were seeking their right to suffrage. Their moment in American history was both racially and sexually charged: The cult of true womanhood dominated the debate for woman suffrage, and lynching emerged as a disciplinary practice for racial and sexual control. Just as discourse about proper gender roles intervened directly in the political battles taking place in the Trial of the Queen and the Women's March to Versailles, we can read the work of Wells and Goldman as they attempted to make progressive political interventions in highly charged debates over which bodies would be deemed suitable for full American citizenship.

Even though the Fifteenth Amendment, ratified in 1870, guaranteed that black men could not be denied the right to vote, southern states enacted discriminatory codes based on such things as literacy and property requirements that severely limited and effectively denied the right of suffrage to black men. The post–Civil War era saw an increase in lynching and mob violence against African American men and women and their supporters in the white community. Punishment outside the law became notoriously extreme and more frequent, just as black males were gaining fragile rights within the law. At the same moment, white women were organizing for the vote, maneuvering within a political context where some found it expedient to claim that granting suffrage to white women would have the beneficial effect of limiting the influence of uneducated black men. Both Wells and Goldman were forced to stake out positions within this highly charged racial and sexual context. Both Goldman's and Wells's positions deserve attention from feminists. They each mark a significant and fascinating divergence from the mainstream position on female suffrage and its relationship to the cult of true womanhood.

Born into slavery and educated by her parents to seek social justice, Wells was stirred by the lynching of three young black businessmen in Memphis into thinking more systematically about the reasons underlying the lynching of African Americans—primarily men but also some women. In her writings, Wells revealed the stereotypes surrounding definitions of black masculinity and white femininity, as well as their accompanying myths concerning black femininity and white masculinity. In addition to her journalistic work for *Free Speech* and *New York Age,* Wells published three pamphlets on lynching (Wells 1997): *Southern Horrors: Lynch Law in All Its Phases, A Red Record,* and *Mob Rule in New Orleans.* She also wrote an autobiography, went on numerous speaking tours around the country—sometimes with Frederick Douglass—and gained international recognition for the antilynching campaign by twice touring and lecturing in the

United Kingdom. Wells was also one of the first and most important black supporters of the vote for women; she is credited with starting the black Clubwomen's movement and was a founder of the National Association for the Advancement of Colored People (NAACP).

Anarchist, activist, and author of the two-volume *Living My Life* as well as numerous essays and pamphlets (discussed in great detail in chapter 5 of this book), Goldman began her political work as part of the radical immigrant anarchist movement but later branched out to forge coalitions with liberal groups around free speech and birth control. As such, her speeches were located within the issues these movements embraced. Goldman traveled the country making speeches about a coalition of political issues: the rights of workers, the perils of war, militarism and patriotism, the rights of women to birth control, the sanctity of free speech, and the evils of organized government. Some of Goldman's most powerful speeches emphasized the contradictory aspects of the nineteenth-century ideology of femininity. Norms of femininity for women prohibited them from the public sphere, playing up their so-called natural qualities as nurturers, mothers, wives, and chaste daughters. Many women's lives failed to conform to this model of femininity. Goldman was especially outspoken on the ways working women and immigrant women fell outside this domestic paradigm. She also repeatedly made reference to women's sexuality. The nineteenth-century good woman was uninterested in sexual pleasure, whereas Goldman made her advocacy of free love and the sexual pleasure of women central to her definition of freedom for women. However, Goldman did not discuss the ways in which the evolving nineteenth-century ideology of femininity positioned black women as "practically anomalies" (Davis 1981, 5).

Intense divisions within the white women's suffrage movement came to the forefront over questions concerning labor, worker's rights, and abolition. When Susan B. Anthony and Elizabeth Cady Stanton narrowed their political focus solely to women's right to vote, questions important to less advantaged women, such as worker's rights and antilynching reform, were left off the agenda of the mainstream suffrage movement. Paula Giddings (1984) noted that in 1890, when the National American Women's Suffrage Association (NAWSA) was formed, they adopted a position of expediency. Giddings quoted from the 1893 NAWSA convention: "Resolved, that without expressing any opinion on the proper qualifications for voting, we call attention to the significant fact that in every State there are more women who can read and write than all Negro voters; more American women who can read and write than all foreign voters; so that the enfranchisement of such women would settle the vexed question of rule by illiteracy whether of home-grown or foreign-born production" (p. 124).

Both Wells and Goldman abhorred this political move, each from their own respective locations. In her lectures on suffrage, Goldman called all such arguments for suffrage elitist, class bound, anti-immigrant and anti-working class. Speaking from her anarchist convictions, Goldman articulated resistance to suffrage based on its characterization as a misleading remedy within a very corrupted state of legal norms. Wells had even more difficult terrain to negotiate. As an educated and highly political African American woman, she was attentive to race and gender questions and was highly influenced by the argument that blacks should have the opportunity to acquire literacy and to develop their talents and abilities for what Jacqueline

Jones Royster (Wells 1997, 23) called the "betterment both of self and of the race." As Royster explained,

> Like other professional women, she [Wells] was challenged to adhere to nineteenth-century standards of "ladyhood," modesty, decorum, and propriety, even as she ventured ever more boldly as an African American woman into male-dominated "public" space. For African American women, the need to maintain feminine decorum was especially trouble-some. The lash of slavery cut deeply. A primary task was to define oneself not just as a "true woman" but as "human," as capable and deserving of human regard. (pp. 22–23)

Wells was up against an ideology that failed to even recognize that black women were human beings. Judith Butler (2004) poignantly expresses the violence inherent in gender norms that refuse to recognize the existence of particular others. As Butler puts it, "To find that you are fundamentally unintelligible (indeed, that the laws of culture and of language find you to be an impossibility) is to find that you have not yet achieved access to the human, to find yourself speaking only and always as if you were human, but with the sense that you are not, to find that your language is hollow, that no recognition is forthcoming because the norms by which recognition takes place are not in your favor." (p. 30)

From their respective positions, both Goldman and Wells challenged the constraints of femininity imposed on women by the idea of the cult of true womanhood. Goldman noted the hypocrisy of these constraints in every social category, and Wells, like Goldman, directly challenged the ideals by her actions within the public sphere. As a black woman, Wells was an even more visible violation of the category of proper femininity, as African American women were not even included in the category of human.

Neither woman believed that granting the vote to women would cure the ills of turn-of-the-century America, and in this they differed significantly from most of the intellectual women of their historical moment. Unlike Wollstonecraft's move to disassociate gender from bodies and Staël's move to use the rhetoric of femininity strategically to the advantage of women, Wells and Goldman carved alternative paths that took them far beyond the demands of femininity as their historical moment defined them. Wells and Goldman departed from Wollstonecraft's and Staël's strategies in that neither worked within the dictates of femininity to expose its constraints and contradictions. Recall that the cult of domesticity and standards of sensibility dominated the discourse on the denial of French women's participation in politics, just as the cult of true womanhood served to put black women beyond the pale of decency and made politics as a practice seemingly inappropriate for white women. Whereas Wollstonecraft and Staël exposed the fault lines of the cult of sensibility from within its confines, both for the queen and for the market women, Goldman and Wells operated from outside these categories to expose elitist and racist assumptions. Goldman's and Well's positions must be considered within the context of the demand for women suffrage, which, though forged in opposition to the ideals of the cult of true womanhood, became increasingly dominated by its dictates.

Though I discuss Goldman's opposition to allegiance with the women suffrage movement in a larger context in chapter 5, devoted to Goldman's life and politics, I recount some of the most important points in this chapter to distinguish her position and her political strategy from that of Wells. In "Woman Suffrage," Goldman (1969f) identified religion—particularly Christianity—war, and the home (i.e.,

"Church, State, and the home") as the primary aspects of the social usurpation of women's freedom. Yet she claimed that only a minority of those who support suffrage do so to be freed from Church, State, and the home. The majority, she said, insist that suffrage "will make her a better Christian and homekeeper, a staunch citizen of the State... thus suffrage is only a means of strengthening the omnipotence of the very gods that woman has served from time immemorial" (p. 197). In making her argument against the potential freedom offered through the right to vote, Goldman questioned the meaning of freedom within the context of American law. She wrote, "Free to starve, free to tramp the highways of this great country, he enjoys universal suffrage, and by that right, he has forged chains about his limbs. The reward that he receives is stringent labor laws prohibiting the right of boycott, of picketing, in fact, of everything, except the right to be robbed of the fruits of his labor. Yet all these disastrous results of the twentieth-century fetich [fetish] have taught woman nothing. But then, woman will purify politics, we are assured" (p. 198).

Goldman (1969f) was quick to point out that the female suffrage movement had done nothing for women of the lower classes. In Idaho, she argued the suffragette "disenfranchised her sister of the street, and declared all women of "lewd character" unfit to vote" (p. 203). In Colorado, "the Puritanism of woman has expressed itself in a more drastic form," Goldman claimed, going on to quote from *Equal Suffrage* by Helen Sumner: "Men of notoriously unclean lives and men connected with saloons have been dropped from politics since women have the vote" (ibid.). The American suffrage movement, as Goldman defined it, has been, "until very recently, altogether a parlor affair, absolutely detached from the economic needs of the people" (p. 207). She chastised Susan

B. Anthony for being not only indifferent but also openly "antagonistic to labor" (ibid.). The "wretched little [suffrage] bill," set in motion by "valiant fighters," will "benefit only a handful of propertied ladies, with absolutely no provision for the vast mass of working women" (p. 206).

In her writings on the lynchings of African Americans and their defenders, Wells also realized the hypocrisy of those who upheld the cult of true womanhood and sought to grant women the vote on behalf of this restrictive ideal. Like Wollstonecraft, Wells demonstrated how particular gender traits are associated with particular bodies, arguing that "lynching encoded several race and gender stereotypes regarding pleasure and desire" (Royster Introduction to Wells 1997, 30). As Royster explained:

> White women were pure, virginal, and uninterested in sexual pleasure. They needed and deserved protection. African American women were wanton, licentious, promiscuous. White men (who had obviously engaged in sexual acts with African American women over the decades, given the range of skin colors among African Americans) could not be accused of raping "bad" women. "Bad," amoral women did not need or deserve protection. African American women, as amoral women, were not capable of providing a moral influence on African American men or anyone else. African American men were lustful beasts who could not be trusted in the company of "good" women, white women. White men were champions of justice in defense of their women and in preservation of "civilization." (ibid.)

In the first pages of "Southern Horrors," published in 1892, Wells connected the acts of lynching with the hypocrisy of ideals of proper femininity and masculinity for whites and blacks. She wrote that "nobody in this section of the country believes the old thread bare lie that Negro men rape white women....If Southern white men are not careful, they will over-reach themselves and public sentiment will have a reaction; a conclusion will then be reached which will be very

damaging to the moral reputation of their women" (Wells 1997, 52). Wells discussed the fact that black men were not accused of raping white women during slavery or during the four years of civil war. This was a new charge, one Wells associated with a backlash against black men gaining some political leverage within American society. The "race question," as she put it, "should be properly designated an earnest inquiry as to the best methods by which religion, science, law, and political power may be employed to excuse injustice, barbarity, and crime done to a people because of race and color" (p. 57). When the victim of rape is a "colored woman," Wells pointed out, there is not a thing done about it. "At the very moment these civilized whites were announcing their determination to "protect their wives and daughters," by murdering Grizzard [a black man taken from jail and lynched for being accused of raping a white woman], a white man was in the same jail for raping eight-year-old Maggie Reese, an Afro-American girl....He was not harmed" (p. 59).

The hypocrisy of this political context whereby whites were said to protect their wives and daughters from dangerously sexual black men vividly illustrates the sexual and racial ideologies at the heart of lynching. Robyn Wiegman (1995, 83) argues that "in the lynch scenario, the stereotypical fascination and abhorrence for blackness is literalized as a competition for masculinity and seminal power....In severing the black male's penis from his body, either as a narrative account or a material act, the mob aggressively denies the patriarchal sign and symbol of the masculine, interrupting the privilege of the phallus and thereby reclaiming, through the perversity of dismemberment, the black male's (masculine) potential for citizenship." Thus, the black male is feminized and disenfranchised simultaneously, the dismemberment becoming necessary due to the black male's danger as a "mythically endowed rapist" (ibid.).

It is important to notice that in contrast to Staël's strategic invocation of the stereotyped feminine and Wollstonecraft's call to disassociate bodies from gender traits, neither Goldman nor Wells invoked feminine characteristics as a way to align women, nor did they disassociate bodies from gender. Instead, they pointed to the effects of ideological and political characterizations of gender categories within their class and race contexts. Each thinker, thus, engaged in demystifying and deconstructing the feminine and masculine ideals from the outside by pointing to the gaps, fissures, and political manipulations of these categories and their material effects.

It is precisely because gender categories are indeterminate that they take on political meaning in various historical and cultural contexts. Joan Scott (1988, 49) has stressed that "*man* and *woman* are at once empty and overflowing categories. They are empty in that they have no ultimate, transcendent meaning; overflowing because even when they appear to be fixed, they still contain within them alternative, denied, or suppressed definitions." Denise Riley (1992, 121) distinguishes levels of indeterminacy that characterize women as a category. These include "the individual indeterminacy (when am I a woman?), the historical indeterminacy (what do 'women' mean, and when?), and the political indeterminacy (what can 'women' do?)." We saw that in the French Revolutionary period, women's revolutionary action did not follow any preconceived patterns of feminine behavior, no matter how defined. When women acted politically, they acted from a number of different axes and with a variety of demands and

expectations; women do not necessarily act solely—though of course women do sometimes act primarily—as women.

Reminded that it is ill advised to seek to firmly fix notions of woman and the female self, women activists and theorists during the French Revolution and during the quest for female suffrage in the United States were faced with politically difficult situations. In *Only Paradoxes to Offer: French Feminists and the Rights of Man*, Joan Scott (1996, xi) explains the dilemma of needing to invoke qualities of group identity even while denying their negative characteristics in terms of a "politics of undecidability." Due to the political situation whereby the Rights of Man were presumed to be universal, yet posited as against and exclusive of women's rights, women were forced to accept definitions of gender to argue on behalf of their sex while maintaining that gender should not matter if rights are indeed universal. Yet the question remains as to when it is politically effective to invoke identity categories, versus when invoking these categories is inherently exclusive of others. Wells recounted in her autobiography (*Crusade for Justice*, 1970) that it was wrong for Susan B. Anthony to deny Frederick Douglass a place at the convention for the Equal Suffrage Association when they met in Atlanta, Georgia. Wells recalled that Anthony justified her exclusion of Douglass as "expedient" because she did not want "to subject him to humiliation" and especially did not want "anything to get in the way of bringing the southern white women into our suffrage association, now that their interest had been awakened" (p. 230). Here, the joining of women, exclusive of black women and black men, for political expediency reinforces the exclusionary and disciplinary status of categories of femininity in ways that Goldman and Wells both warned against.

In the following chapters, discussing the ways norms of femininity have constrained the lives of feminist intellectuals, I demonstrate that joining together as women need not be an exclusive or disciplinary move. In contrast, women can come together in coalition to politically reinterpret the meanings of the category. We might unite, I suggest, to protest the demands of femininity that are race and class bound and serve to limit feminist coalition. Recognition of these demands, and how they limit our freedom, is the first step toward challenging them.

3. Women's Situation, II

Existential Experiments with the Feminine

Each of the feminist intellectual's lives whose work I engage in this book can be read as demonstrating what Beauvoir identifies as claiming freedom within situation; in many cases, this freedom is nourished and enabled by the privilege their situation confers. The privilege they enjoy(ed) might include material wealth and status, whiteness, or the privilege of being in an intellectual position to influence political contexts or to shape and define their own intellectual legacy. Within their feminist writing, theory, and political work, they each called attention to and sought to ameliorate the damaging effects of material conditions of femininity and the political divisions witnessed by differences among women. Even so, they had difficulty creating the conditions in which they could live their feminist aspirations and make it possible for other women to do the same. Often, the norms of femininity were so deeply ingrained in their consciousness that they sometimes read traditional feminine traits in either misogynist (e.g., Mary Wollstonecraft) or valorized ways (e.g., Germaine de Staël; at times Emma Goldman).

The Construction of Desire

One of the most interesting observations of *The Second Sex* I draw on throughout this book—and one seen in the study of Wollstonecraft's analysis of her own relationship to the market women—is that women's subjective response to being placed in the position of Other is often problematic, even when that woman is a feminist.

Though she does not cite Simone de Beauvoir, Nancy Hirschmann (2003) described the internalization of oppression and the social construction of desire in a similar way. Hirschmann studied women's lived experiences, such as battery, receiving welfare, and veiling, to describe how the choosing subject comes to be constructed by her contexts, or what Beauvoir called situation. As Hirschmann put it, "the 'choosing subject' exists within and is framed by particular contexts, contexts which for the most part exhibit varying degrees and forms of gender hierarchy and oppression" (p. x).

Beauvoir (1989, xxv) made it explicit that even for independent women, desire is socially constructed. Women's desires are constructed within a world in which they lack concrete means for organization, material resources, and economic independence and are tied to their oppressors—through family, economics, and subjective need—"more firmly than they are to other women." The historical and embodied specificity of each woman's situation, moreover, often serves to weaken bonds of women across race and class boundaries. In the previous chapter, the difficulty of creating ties of women's solidarity across class boundaries in the French Revolution and across race and class boundaries in early twentieth-century American politics were made explicit. In addition, Beauvoir theorized that throughout their lives, women are taught to aspire to norms of femininity specific to their race and class location. These norms are created and enforced by oppressors and peers alike—both men and women.

In Book One of *The Second Sex*, Beauvoir (1989) documented the "facts and myths" of biology, history, and literature that have served to conceptualize woman as Other. This history plays a substantive material role in women's lived reality and her psychological desires and fantasies. Beauvoir poses this pressing question in her introduction: "Why is it that women do not dispute male sovereignty?" (p. xxiv). Her response, articulated throughout *The Second Sex*, meshes subjective response with material forces. As Beauvoir put it, we must describe "woman such as men have fancied her in their dreams, for what-in-men's-eyes-she-seems-to-be is one of the necessary factors in her real situation" (p. 138).

This analysis, linking subjective and objective circumstances, provides a much-needed alternative to the well-trodden equality-versus-difference debates that have dominated feminist intellectual discussion. The dilemma as constructed by the equality–difference debate is posed as: achieving equality with men measures women's accomplishments and desires in male terms, while acknowledging difference ghettoizes women within the characteristics that served to subordinate them in the first place. Beauvoir's emphasis on embodiment, freedom, and situation predates and reinforces contemporary feminist efforts to move beyond the false choice between equality and difference, gender construction versus bodily essentialism. When we think from the perspective of Beauvoir's emphasis on situation and embodiment, the Wollstonecraft–Staël debate over the political significance of the trial and execution of Marie-Antoinette and the treacherous battle for women's suffrage in early twentieth-century America require a more complex understanding of the relationship between gendered bodies and their social–political significance. These moments cannot be fully understood from within the dichotomous opposition between male equality and female difference. The social construction of masculinity and femininity and its relationship to particular classed and raced bodies demand a focus on the political significance of embodiment within any given specific context. By specifying situation and embodiment, Beauvoir asks us to recognize the political dimensions of oppressive material norms that are fully bound with class, race, and compulsory heterosexuality. At the same time, her work makes it possible to recognize how consciousness of these categories can help us to work against them and to create political coalitions with others.

Judith Butler's (1993) question concerning "whether recourse to matter and to the materiality of sex is necessary in order to establish that irreducible specificity that is said to ground feminist practice" (p. 29) is answered by Beauvoir. With Butler, Beauvoir (1989) recognizes that bodies matter and that gender norms are material, while simultaneously noting their constructive and performative possibilities. Neither thinker seeks to ground feminist practice within the materiality of bodies, yet neither denies embodiment. The point for both, as I interpret the significance of their insights in common, is to explore how—when certain norms of femininity become sedimented—feminists might imagine and reinvent new ways of becoming and being women. As Beauvoir famously put it, "If her functioning as a female is not enough to define woman, if we decline also to explain her through 'the eternal feminine,' and if nevertheless we admit, provisionally, that women do exist, then we must face the question: what is a woman?"

(p. xxi). This is *the* question of *The Second Sex*. Beauvoir immediately remarked that to ask this question in itself is significant: "If I wish to define myself, I must first of all say: 'I am a woman'; on this truth must be based all further discussion" (ibid.). Using her own life and the lives of other women as concrete examples, Beauvoir utilized existential phenomenology to focus on individual cases—in this instance, of women's struggles toward freedom.

Staking out the claim that her goal in *The Second Sex* is to explore the particular question of what a woman is and how she might be defined, Beauvoir (1989) admitted that it is inherently difficult to discover the answer.

> Man is at once judge and party to the case; but so is woman. What we need is an angel—neither man nor woman—but where shall we find one? Still, the angel would be poorly qualified to speak, for an angel is ignorant of all the basic facts involved in the problem. With a hermaphrodite we should be no better off, for here the situation is most peculiar; the hermaphrodite is not really the combination of a whole man and a whole woman, but consists of parts of each and thus is neither. It looks to me as if there are, after all, certain women who are best qualified to elucidate the situation of woman. (p. xxxiii)

Significantly, Beauvoir argued that she is uniquely qualified to elucidate the situation of women. In answering that she is a woman, in response to the question "what is a woman?" Beauvoir claimed to count herself among women (Bauer 2001, 46–77). Here, she did not intend to rise above women as an exceptional woman. She claimed, instead, that she was a woman with other women. Among women, even women radically different from herself, Beauvoir described experiences that illuminate the political, social, economic, and psychological significance of being a woman in the world alongside the awareness that each woman is always also a unique and particular individual. As Patricia Moynagh (2006, 21) explains, "Beauvoir's position is this: she wants to claim her sexed existence, but not be defined exclusively by it. Beauvoir puts it this way: 'my feminine status...is a given condition of my life, not an explanation of it' (*Prime of Life*, 292). This is why she finds it unjust if she is reduced to her sex. On the other hand, trying to remove herself from her sexed existence is not a 'good faith' option because doing so would deny her 'subjective self.'"

I find it most significant that Beauvoir demonstrated her own situation as an upper-class, intellectual, white French woman[1] as illuminating issues of political importance for analyzing the significance of women's situation within patriarchal conditions that vary widely across cultural, racial, and class boundaries. Hirschmann (2003, 174) reminds us that "as has been documented by many, Western feminists too frequently treat women in different cultures [and we might add, in different situations and contexts] as if they were simply variations on a basic theme defined by white, Western, middle-class experience." In identifying herself as a woman and in seeking to locate the significance of sexual difference in the lived experiences of women—even women very unlike her—I interpret Beauvoir as emphasizing the importance of recognizing difference within herself and among others. Sonia Kruks (2001, 6–7) characterizes the existential perspective as employing "the deliberate and intentional use of the concrete as a way of approaching the abstract, the particular as a way of approaching the general." Carla Hesse (2001, 149) notes, "If Beauvoir is most typically remembered as a singular woman, alone the equal among men, it is only because we have now forgotten the deep cultural influences she derived from her avid reading of earlier women writers." Indeed, in *The Second Sex*, as well as in her autobiography and her novels, Beauvoir specifically looked to the lives of particular women—including herself—as a way to understand the lives and situations of women within hierarchically gendered social–political structures. She found that to understand her own experience she needed to first examine the fact that she was a woman and thus experienced the world subjectively and objectively in ways highly influenced by norms of femininity. As Nancy Bauer (2001, 200) explains, "The constraints on women Beauvoir refers to summed up by the idea that their "being-for-men" is an essential part of their lives, are to be seen as constraints on Beauvoir herself."

In keeping with the existentialist approach where the particular is used as a way of approaching the general, Beauvoir announced that her own case proves instructive. Beauvoir's experience as an intellectual woman, considered with the experiences of other independent and free-thinking women, is especially helpful to examine in thinking through women's situation under patriarchal social–political conditions. Beauvoir interpreted her own subjective experience to find that her life, though openly and consciously defying the dictates of the demands of femininity, was still the life of a woman. Her life experience contradicted the general category of woman as defined by male versions of the feminine, but her lived reality was still that of a sexually different human being. Here we find the opposite of the philosophical rule, as according to a philosopher such as Plato. Rather than subsume her life under the universal, essential category of woman, Beauvoir displayed her life to show that the category as constructed by men fails to exist. Herein, her life as a woman is a particular life that reveals a general truth. Along these lines, Karen Vintges (1996, 148) has argued that Beauvoir made "philosophy out of her own experiences." Vintges adds that this "truth in subjective experience" can "offer comfort to others because it breaks down the boundaries of individuality" (p. 149). Interpreting Beauvoir, Moynagh (2006, 26) argues that "while retaining their specificity, her examples must address the more general conditions shaping women's lives." As Moynagh (ibid.) elaborates: "This is Beauvoir's dialogic pitch to her audience: Do you see your life or other women's lived experiences depicted in the examples I present to you? Do you see something of yourself or others in my struggles even though we are worlds apart?"

The entire second half—Book Two—of Beauvoir's *Second Sex* is devoted to descriptive passages of women's lived reality understood as the ways in which women comprehend and then attempt to negotiate their freedom within situation. As Beauvoir (1989, xxxv) remarked, "The drama of woman lies in this conflict between the fundamental aspirations of every subject (ego)—who always regards the self as the essential—and the compulsions of a situation in which she is the inessential. How can a human being in woman's situation attain fulfillment? What roads are open to her? Which are blocked? How can independence be recovered in a state of dependency?" Notice how Beauvoir attended to context and situation here. She spoke of the fundamental aspirations of the subject always recognizing that the subject is constructed within situation. For Beauvoir, freedom was defined positively as a reaching out toward the other—a relationship that entails freedom's essential linkage to responsibility.[2] Thus, every subject's freedom is understood within her situation, and one person cannot decide what another person's freedom may entail. The problem Beauvoir articulated as a lack of freedom is the subject's definition as inessential. Beauvoir's theoretical context allows for the fact that another woman's freedom may look differently from my own; to demand freedom for women does not include defining the positive characteristics of what that freedom entails or saving them from their own misguided sense of what freedom looks like. This latter sense of knowing the content of freedom's specific actualization can be characterized by the notion that Western feminism is the ultimate prototype and arbiter of feminism's potential. Not only does this assume that feminism is indeed always "Western"; it also fails to recognize that there may be different ideas of freedom within varying situations that women can choose for themselves once freed from their designation as the "inessential," to use Beauvoir's terms. What is most important in my reading of Beauvoir's notion of potential freedom within situation is the recognition of oppression and the demand that the subject be given the room to be called to personhood, so to speak, within a plurality of other free beings.

The categories considered by Beauvoir (1989) as the contexts and moments within which women are called to personhood under patriarchal conditions include "The Formative Years" (i.e., "Childhood," "The Young Girl," "Sexual Initiation," "The Lesbian"); "Situation" (i.e., "The Married Woman," "The Mother," "Social Life," "Prostitutes and Hetairas," "From Maturity to Old Age," "Women's Situation and Character"); "Justifications" (i.e., "The Narcissist," "The Woman in Love," "The Mystic"); and "Toward Liberation" (i.e., "The Independent Woman"). To probe the constraints on the feminist thinkers explored in this work, I am informed by all these categories, but for now I focus briefly on chapter 25, titled "The Independent Woman." I want to linger on this chapter for a moment because the women I study in this book are not ordinary but rather are intellectual, feminist, women. Beauvoir described the situation of such women in the following passage:

> There are, however, a fairly large number of privileged women who find in their professions a means of economic and social autonomy. These come to mind when one considers woman's possibilities and her future. This is the reason why it is especially interesting to make a close study of their situation, even though they constitute as yet only a minority; they continue to be a subject of debate between feminists and antifeminists. The latter assert that the emancipated women of today succeed in doing nothing of importance in the world and that furthermore they have difficulty in achieving their own inner equilibrium. The former exaggerate the results obtained by professional women and are blind to their inner confusion. (p. 681)

It is the interpretation Beauvoir offers in light of the comments of those she calls the "feminists" in this passage that interests me here. Beauvoir commented that feminists "exaggerate the results obtained by professional women and are blind to their inner confusion." As she elaborated, even when a woman is in an independent economic position and is consciously seeking her freedom, "when she begins her adult life she doesn't have behind her the same past as does a boy; she is not viewed by society in the same way; the universe presents itself to her in a different perspective" (p. 682). Therefore, "the fact of being a woman today poses peculiar problems for an independent human individual" (ibid.).

There is a peculiar conundrum confronting the independent woman. Because women are taught that being feminine entails denouncing freedom, the woman who seeks to claim her freedom finds that to do so she must renounce her femininity. Put in practical terms, "desire for a feminine destiny—husband, home, children—and the enchantment of love are not always easy to reconcile with the will to succeed" (Beauvoir 1989, 703). As Beauvoir explained further, "It is this conflict that especially marks the situation of the emancipated woman. She refuses to confine herself to her role as female, because she will not accept mutilation; but it would also be a mutilation to repudiate her sex" (p. 682). Must a woman become a man to enjoy the privileges of humanity? Beauvoir refused this option, yet she also refused the option of embracing femininity as delineated by the demands of femininity specific to one's racial, class, historical, and cultural location. Embracing this version of femininity necessarily entails a renunciation of freedom—an act of bad faith. Society places the emancipated woman in this double bind. Beauvoir exclaimed that "misogynists have often reproached intellectual women for 'neglecting themselves'; but they have also preached this doctrine to them: if you wish to be our equals, stop using make-up and nail-polish" (ibid.). Emancipated women judge their success by the standards of the demands of femininity specific to their location.

> It is not regard for the opinion of others alone that leads her to give time and care to her appearance and her housekeeping. She wants to retain her womanliness for her own satisfaction. She can regard herself with approval throughout her present and past only in combining the life she has made for herself with the destiny that her mother, her childhood games, and her adolescent fantasies prepared for her. She has entertained narcissistic dreams; to the male's phallic pride she still opposes her cult of self; she wants to be seen, to be attractive....Obedient to the feminine tradition, she will wax her floors and she will do her own cooking instead of going to eat at a restaurant as a man would in her place. She wants to live at once like a man and like a woman, and in that way she multiplies her tasks and adds to her fatigue. (p. 684)

Beauvoir's passages specifically on the intellectual woman are worth quoting at length:

The independent woman—and above all the intellectual, who thinks about her situation—will suffer, as a female, from an inferiority complex; she lacks leisure for such minute beauty care as that of the coquette whose sole aim in life is to be seductive; follow the specialists' advice as she may, she will never be more than an amateur in the domain of elegance. Feminine charm demands that transcendence, degraded into immanence, appear no longer as anything more than a subtle quivering of the flesh; it is necessary to be spontaneously offered prey. But the intellectual knows that she is offering herself, she knows that she is a conscious being, a subject; one can hardly dull one's glance and change one's eyes into sky-blue pools at will; one does not infallibly stop the surge of a body that is straining toward the world and change it into a statue animated by vague tremors. The intellectual woman will try all the more zealously because she fears failure; but her conscious zeal is still an activity and it misses its goal....Thus in imitating abandon the intellectual woman becomes tense...over her blankly naïve face, there suddenly passes a flash of all-too-sharp intelligence; lips soft with promise suddenly tighten....As soon as she feels awkward, she becomes vexed at her abjectness; she wants to take her revenge by playing the game with masculine weapons: she talks instead of listening, she displays subtle thoughts, strange emotions; she contradicts the man instead of agreeing with him, she tries to get the best of him. Mme de Staël won some resounding victories: she was almost irresistible. (p. 685)

As I demonstrate through letters, memoir, autobiographical fiction, and various other forms and moments of self-revelation, each of the feminist intellectuals I discuss in the pages of this book has experienced the dilemmas of the intellectual woman Beauvoir writes of. Throughout the book, the conundrum of desiring and attempting to claim freedom while still enjoying the specific kind of fulfillment promised to women is painfully experienced by each thinker as an inability to forge a path toward freedom as a woman. The feminist intellectual knows she is a subject, yet she is seen in the world as an object: as one needing to conform to the demands of femininity as dictated by her social location or be chastised. Complicating things

further, the feminist woman has desires that sometimes conform to—
and are certainly influenced by—the demands of femininity. She may
want love, the bonds of intimacy, and perhaps motherhood defined
in precisely the ways her social location dictates. Or she may refuse
some or all of these and, in doing so, may create alternatives to these
kinds of bonds that remain outside the norm. Can these feminine
traits, even when recreated, be reconciled with the accomplishments
of the free subject? How must bonds of intimacy be reinvented to
prevent them from circumscribing the freedom of the subject? Might
both freedom and intimacy be reimagined in articulating new ways
of being a woman?

Embracing Ambiguity

Beauvoir's turn to particular examples is illuminating, particularly in
the context of her philosophical insights. Recall that Beauvoir's conception of freedom is deeply related to situation and that to her freedom is never experienced alone. In *The Ethics of Ambiguity*, Beauvoir
(1976, 9) urged us, as subjects, to "assume our fundamental ambiguity." Though human beings are individual subjects ethically compelled to assume our freedom, this sort of individualism does not lead
to "the anarchy of personal whim" (p. 156). The individual "is defined
only by his relationship to the world and to other individuals; he exists
only by transcending himself, and his freedom can be achieved only
through the freedom of others" (ibid.). Thus, freedom for the subject
never entails acting outside the boundaries of responsibility and of
respect for other subjects in the world.

This view of freedom, which recognizes the ambiguity of the
human subject—that we are at once subject and object—defies the

construction of the subject as masculine and the object as feminine. Our lived reality reveals the fundamental ambiguity of human existence for both sexes, yet, as Beauvoir (1989) claimed, we continually engage in attempts to deny this ambiguity. Due again to situation, men are more readily able to deny their ambiguity in a sexual situation.

> Men and women all feel the shame of their flesh; in its pure, inactive presence, its unjustified immanence, the flesh exists, under the gaze of others, in its absurd contingence, and yet it is *oneself*: oh, to prevent it from existing for others, oh, to deny it! There are men who say they cannot bear to show themselves naked before a woman unless in a state of erection; and indeed through erection the flesh becomes activity, potency, the sex organ is not long an inert object, but like the hand or face, the imperious expression of a subjectivity. (p. 381)

Further exploring how the dominant construction of masculinity is defined through a radical subjectivity that denies ambiguity, Beauvoir turned to a particular case, exemplified in the life and the literature of the Marquis de Sade. Though she was ultimately to reject Sade's project as failing to provide an ethical framework to negotiate relationships between self and other, initially Beauvoir (1953, 80) found Sade's project attractive in that it takes a stand against "abstractions and alienations." The abstractions and alienations Sade rejected were those of bourgeois individuality and abstract universalism. Beauvoir liked that Sade had no use for a universalism whereby men become a "mere collection of objects" rather than a "universe peopled with individual beings" (p. 26). She was also attracted to Sade's sincere attempt to make his "psycho-physical destiny an ethical choice," noting his question to be: "Can we, without renouncing our individuality, satisfy our aspirations to universality?" (p. 12).

Beauvoir had long been interested in ethical questions concerning how individuals, separated from others in the world through freedom and finitude, might come together with others in community and solidarity. In 1944, writing in *Pyrrhus and Cineas* about the conflicting dimensions of inter-subjective life, Beauvoir wrote that "humanity is a discontinuous succession of free men who are irretrievably isolated by their subjectivity" (2004, 109). When she turned to the work and life of Sade, she was interested to see whether he might have insight into the question of how individuals might retain their distinctiveness yet come together in a community. In contrast to abstract rules that fail to recognize the concrete particularity of individual freedoms, Sade's devotion to sexual violence might be seen as a respect for human flesh. Initially Beauvoir considered this possibility: "In order to derive pleasure from the humiliation and exaltation of the flesh, one must ascribe value to the flesh. It has no sense, no worth, once one casually begins to treat man as a thing" (1953, 26).

However, Beauvoir found that ultimately Sade could not offer any solution to the fundamental ambiguity of the human condition that she had articulated in 1948 in these terms: "that he [man] is at the same time a freedom and a thing, both unified and scattered, isolated by his subjectivity and nevertheless coexisting at the heart of the world with other men" (2004, 258). Sade's project failed, according to Beauvoir, due to an unrestrained desire, a kind of abandonment to radical subjectivity that failed to recognize the reality of other human beings in the world, each in their own subjectivity. Beauvoir quotes Sade as saying: "What does one want when one is engaged in the sexual act? That everything about you give you its utter attention, think only of you, care only for you . . . every man wants to be a tyrant when he fornicates" (1953, 16). In desiring this complete tyranny, an "illusion of power," whereby he would become the "lone and sovereign feudal despot" (ibid.), Sade could not recognize that others exist in the world in their own subjectivity.

For Beauvoir, to fail to recognize others in their own fundamental ambiguity is to fail at your own freedom. She put it quite simply by stating that "we need others in order for our own existence to become founded and necessary" (2004, 129). Clarifying further, Beauvoir stated: "So here is my situation facing others: men are free, and I am thrown into the world among these foreign freedoms. I need them because once I have surpassed my own goals, my actions will fall back upon themselves, inert and useless, if they have not been carried off toward a new future by new projects" (2004, 135). Hence, "respect for the other's freedom is not an abstract rule. It is the first condition of my successful effort. I can only appeal to the other's freedom, not constrain it" (2004, 136). While Sade may value his own freedom at the highest level, and reject the rules of abstract universalism whereby we all become a "mere collection of objects" (1953, 26), his own radical embrace of subjectivity disallowed him from the recognition of the subjectivity of others. What he failed to recognize is that we are all subjects and objects, in ourselves, and in community.

When Beauvoir discusses the condition of ambiguity of human beings in terms of gender construction, she makes it quite clear that masculinity is a training for subjectivity, while femininity is its opposite. Beauvoir (1989, 371) noted that men are taught to deny their ambiguity, and to project their freedom outward into the world as subjects:

For a man, the transition from childish sexuality to maturity is relatively simple: erotic pleasure is objectified, desire being directed toward another person instead of being realized within the bounds of self. Erection is the expression of this need; with penis, hands, mouth, with his whole body, a man reaches out toward his partner, but he himself remains at the center of this activity, being, on the whole, the *subject* as opposed to *objects* he perceives and *instruments* that he manipulates; he projects himself toward the other without losing his independence; the feminine flesh is for him a prey, and through it he gains access to the qualities he desires, as with any object.

Trained for manhood, Sade advocated treating other people as "things," failing to grasp the reality of their situations, failing to experience the "emotional intoxication" (Beauvoir 1953, 32), only possible when viewing the other as a subject. As Beauvoir explained:

The state of emotional intoxication allows one to grasp existence in one's self and in the other, as both subjectivity and passivity. The two partners merge in this ambiguous unity; each one is freed of his own presence and achieves immediate communication with the other. The curse which weighed upon Sade—and which only his childhood would explain—was this "autism" which prevented him from ever forgetting himself or being genuinely aware of the reality of the other person. (pp. 32–33)

Turning to this specific example of the life and work of the Marquis de Sade, Beauvoir argued that a life lived as sovereign subject fails to assume any ethical dimensions. In denying the reality of other people in their subjectivity and ambiguity, Sade makes himself a tyrant rather than an authentically free subject.

In contrast, Beauvoir (1989, 372) argued that women's "eroticism is much more complex," reflecting the ambiguity of their situation. It would be better put, though, to argue that the construction of the dominant conceptions of masculinity and femininity align with the philosophical and political constructions of subject and object, respectively, and these are deeply connected to situation. Men, too, often cannot attain the subjectivity required for the kind of manliness expected of them as sovereign subjects and must rely on outside help, whether from people (as objects) or actual physical objects. Judith Halberstam (2002), for example, finds that "epic masculinity," by which she means the masculinity of the white male, depends on a host of accoutrements and is primarily prosthetic. Analyzing a James Bond film, Halberstam argues that epic masculinity depends absolutely on "a vast subterranean network of secret government troops, well-funded scientists, the army, and an endless supply of both beautiful bad babes and beautiful good babes, and finally it relies heavily on an immediately recognizable 'bad guy'" (p. 357). A study of female masculinity, in contrast, demonstrates for Halberstam that sexism and misogyny need not be "necessarily part and parcel of masculinity, even though historically it has become difficult, if not impossible, to untangle masculinity from the oppression of women" (ibid.).

I cite Halberstam's (2002) work here to again highlight the focus on situation. The performance of gender must be considered within situation as Beauvoir described it. Though Beavuoir (1989) spoke of men's and women's situation as characterized by the positions of subject and object, she argued that men and women are socialized into these polar opposites, a socialization that denies the fundamental ambiguity of every individual as comprising both positions. We can see that owning the attributes of masculinity and femininity, as subject and object respectively, is decidedly more complicated when we consider alternative situations in which men and women find or place themselves. Butler (2004, 213), for example, refers to her own younger years when she lived as a "bar dyke." She claims that femininity never really "belonged" to her; when it "quickly dawned" on her that some "so-called men could do femininity much better that [she] ever could, ever wanted to, ever would," she was "confronted by what can only be called the transferability of the attribute" (ibid.) The important point for Butler is that feminism should be committed to the ideal that "no one should be forcibly compelled to occupy a gender norm that is undergone, experientially, as an unlivable violation" (ibid.).

We might add to Butler's insight that it is an unlivable violation to have to be the sovereign subject or the ruled object all the time. Hence, the tragedy of a failure to recognize ambiguity.

Beauvoir (1989) consistently emphasized the ethical potential in recognizing the fundamental ambiguity of every human being. She argued that the thinking woman's situation—experiencing herself as object though knowing herself as free subject—strikingly reveals the ambiguity of the human condition and the potential for ethical relationships.

> Sex pleasure in woman, as I have said, is a kind of magic spell; it demands complete abandon; if words or movements oppose the magic of caresses, the spell is broken....As we have seen, she wants to remain subject while she is made object. Being more profoundly beside herself than is man because her whole body is moved by desire and excitement, she retains her subjectivity only through union with her partner; giving and receiving must be combined for both. (p. 397)

The consciousness of women's situation, that which is felt and thought particularly keenly by intellectual women, might lead to an alternative. As reflected in the lengthy passages I quoted earlier, Beauvoir (1989) argued that intellectual women think about their situation as free subjects in the world, though they are seen as objects by men, particularly in sexual situations. This reflection on the fundamental ambiguity of human beings, which is more apparent to particular women due to their situation, leads us out of the dualities presented by the conflict between, for example, thinking as a feminist and being seen as a woman. As Bauer (2001, 226) puts it, "What is required for reciprocal recognition on Beauvoir's view is the willingness and the wherewithal to make oneself both subject and object in the other's eyes." Were we to become conscious of and recognize this fundamental ambiguity of human beings, could not one be both a feminist and a woman—affirming myriad ways to be a woman outside the constraints of the demands of femininity—simultaneously?

Feminist Consciousness

Finally, I want to emphasize the importance of articulating a feminist consciousness through a collective political process of claiming freedom. Beauvoir (1989, 627) argued repeatedly that though women are encouraged by the construct of what she called the eternal feminine to remain passive, "resignedness is only abdication and flight, there is no other way out for woman than to work for her liberation." The individual woman will never be able to do this alone. As Beauvoir insisted, "liberation must be collective" (ibid.). To identify what women do and do not have in common across our many differences can be gained through a better understanding of women's situation—particularly the situation of our feminist predecessors as linked through feminist genealogy. This consciousness makes no claims to speak for women or on their behalf but rather with and among women in our diversity. As I emphasized earlier in this chapter, the content of freedom, the look of freedom, can never be specified in advance. The kind of feminist consciousness I call for in this book recognizes that women in radically dissimilar kinds of situations might have different ideas about freedom, such as, for example, Islamic women's struggle to open up spaces for freedom consistent with their religious beliefs. This is not a call for a simplistic version of cultural relativism.[3] Rather, it is a recognition, even an embrace, of the fact that we exist in plurality. As Beauvoir articulated it: "I am dealing not with one freedom but with *several* freedoms. And precisely because they are free, they do not agree among themselves. Kantian ethics enjoins me to seek the support of all humanity, but we have seen that there exists no heaven where the reconciliation of human judgments is accomplished" (2004, 131). We must engage in the work necessary to begin to articulate that women should not be denied substantive freedom nor defined by someone else as an object or as inessential. Yet, we also must acknowledge that women do not all want the same things, even when they have a feminist consciousness.

I argue that studying the lives and theory of particular feminist intellectuals and illuminating situation, consciousness, and ambiguity reveal certain fundamental insights concerning women's relationship to constraints of femininity and their struggles to assume freedom. The feminists I study are engaged in a project of critically reflecting on their experiences and the social, historical, and political context from which they arise. They reflect on these experiences and situations in terms of what it means for them to be women in the world who desire something beyond what the norms of femininity have to offer. At the same time, they know themselves to be women, objectified in the world as well as experiencing their own subjectivity in ways they recognize as influenced by the demands of femininity. In light of this, they seek to transform these norms by the very act of living their lives in alternative ways. Each feminist intellectual I study here offers up her own life and work as example.

Autobiographical and biographical knowledge, when considered alongside theoretical work, allows us to engage these feminists in ways that help us to understand more about the situation of women and the potential for feminist consciousness. To think through these questions, I focus on Beauvoir's philosophical use of examples, especially from her own life and experiences. As demonstrated in *The Second Sex*, Beauvoir (1989) presents hundreds of examples from women's lives. Her sources include autobiographies, memoirs, letters and diaries, conversations with friends, anecdotes, her own life, and archival and library research into the lives of women. This turn to the prolific use of examples is intentional; it is a methodological tool employed to delineate the lives of particular women to learn about the lives of women in general (see Moynagh 2006). This method serves to illuminate autobiographical moments in women's lives, helping us to see within the particular something that is valuable for more than one case.[4] Focusing especially on existential experiments with claiming freedom, these exemplary moments connect us to the situation of women generally.

In looking to the examples of feminist intellectuals to reflect on their lives and work, I do not offer here a model for an identity-based political solution. These lives are not intended for valorization but rather for study and inspiration. I hope that my focus on the particular lives and reflections on them help us rethink the relationship between universal and particular, equality and difference. While these lives clearly invalidate the notion of a universal ideal of woman and the eternal feminine, they simultaneously demonstrate that these women do not live their lives just like men. Their particular situations verify the truth of their lived reality as feminists who defy the demands of femininity, yet are defined through and constrained by structures and ideas thoroughly permeated by heterosexual and specific gender norms.

Each woman in this book is highly cognizant of the fact that to solely affirm one's identity is not to affect significant structural change. As singular examples, these lives reveal that no woman can nor should forge a path toward freedom solely on her own. The feminist work I present here demonstrates that women's liberation must be a collective effort. I read these feminist lives and struggles as examples to raise feminist consciousness. Kruks (2001, 104) credits an insight of Frantz Fanon's in remarking that "affirmation of identity can be liberating *only* in the context of a struggle also to transform wider material and institutional forms of oppression." Here, the work of feminist genealogy becomes most valuable. When we look at feminist lives, complete with satisfactions and triumphs as well as failures and disappointments, we are connected genealogically to the worlds of women whose work and lives can become an inspiration for our own. Precisely because they were intellectuals and, hence, thought about the significance of their lives and work, they can offer possible collective solutions to the situation of contemporary women. Focusing on their work, then, does not serve to obscure the lives of ordinary women but rather to illuminate them. Because these women intellectuals are feminists, with collective liberation as their goal, their reflections on the significance of sexual difference—their own as well as that of women highly unlike themselves—serve as exemplary, pointing beyond their singular lives.

4. Love in Exile

Reading the Memoirs of Mary Wollstonecraft and Germaine de Staël

You will ask, perhaps, why I wished to go further northward. Why?...I want faith! My imagination hurries me forward to seek an asylum in such a retreat from all the disappointments I am threatened with.

Mary Wollstonecraft, *A Short Residence in Sweden, Norway, and Denmark* (1796)

I wept, not for liberty—it had never existed in France—but for the hope of it, which had been enough to exalt the soul for over ten years.

Germaine de Staël, *Ten Years of Exile* (1821)

An unfulfilled desire for revolutionary change, in politics as well as domesticity, haunts the pages of the travel memoirs of Mary Wollstonecraft and Germaine de Staël. These women were roughly contemporaries, though never collaborators. As we saw in chapter 2, they each witnessed the most hopeful as well as the most tragic events of the French Revolution. Putting the concerns and lives of women at the center of their work, each writer proclaimed a personal investment in the Revolution's outcome and was profoundly disappointed by the implications of its failure. In this chapter, I focus specifically on Wollstonecraft's (1987) *A Short Residence in Sweden, Norway, and Denmark,* published in 1796, and Staël's (2001) *Ten Years of Exile,* published in 1821. I read these two memoirs to engage Wollstonecraft's and Staël's existential experiments with femininity and document the ways political events affected their lives as women and as feminists.

The French Revolution occupies a central space in each author's memoir as metaphor for political possibility as well as unfulfilled promise. Amidst the French Revolution's initial euphoria, both reasoned that women would share in the benefits accorded to French citizens. Once it became clear that in the newly created definition of citizenship, *woman* and *citizen* would be construed as irreconcilable categories, Wollstonecraft's and Staël's early hopes gave way to disillusionment. From their differing perspectives, each contributed to the debate concerning women's role in politics and society, and in her own way each sought to alleviate gender inequity. For both Wollstonecraft and Staël, then, writing the travel memoir served as a vehicle through which to express the circumstances of their lives as intellectual women and to respond to and analyze political events in which both were deeply and inextricably engaged.

Both women's journeys were a direct response to political events. Wollstonecraft left England in December 1792 to search for revolutionary ideals in France; in 1795 she journeyed again, this time to Sweden and Norway to search for lost cargo and recover her faith in humanity. Staël was forced from France by Napoleon Bonaparte in 1803. By this time, Staël's novels and essays had earned her great fame, and Napoleon feared her growing influence, her criticism of his regime in the press and its influence on public opinion. The accounts of Wollstonecraft's journeys and Staël's exile document the melancholy that threatened to devour their hope for political change as the various stages of the French Revolution repeatedly disappointed the aspirations of its women.

In the late eighteenth century, to achieve freedom as a woman was to be both a new woman and to achieve something remarkable. Geneviève Fraisse (1994, 103) argues, "A woman's entry into public life and the recognition of her freedom in matters of love were signs of danger because they comprised the two arenas where a woman could achieve autonomy as an individual." Fraisse describes the exceptional woman as one who consciously transgresses norms. Employing Fraisse's definition, Wollstonecraft and Staël were each exceptional women. At the same time, these women are exemplary. While consciously transgressing norms, their struggles with expectations and norms for women illuminate the political and social situation women faced at this historical moment. Struggling to radically reinvent traditional forms of love and politics, these prominent women faced external obstacles and endured personal suffering. Bonnie Smith (1996, 1061) wrote of Staël that she "claimed historical genius for women and herself, showing both for better and for worse how it operated." Wollstonecraft, too, had to grapple with her status as unconventional woman, female intellectual, and social pariah, hoping all the while for reconciliation between women's exceptionality and the possibilities of love. In short, while working toward the goal of improving the lives of women more generally, Wollstonecraft and Staël hoped also to transform political and social life to make room for women like themselves.

Wollstonecraft's Letters

By 1796, Wollstonecraft's early hopes, both for women's education as well as for new structures that would allow her to live a freer life, had been severely tempered. Wollstonecraft's voice in the 1796 *A Short Residence in Sweden, Norway, and Denmark* fits very uncomfortably with our image of her as a strong woman who abhorred the excess sentimentality of the eighteenth-century woman writer and who, as seen in the previous chapter, advocated equality with men as the standard for women. Wollstonecraft's letters were penned after it was clear that women were completely shut out of public life in France. In 1793, the Revolutionary Convention banned all women's clubs, and began their attack on the Society of Revolutionary Republican Women; by the end of 1796, "the term *female citizen* smacked of vulgarity" (Godineau 1998, 368, italics in original). Reflecting on her dashed hopes, Wollstonecraft's private letters are shot through with melancholy, regret, and personal and political doubts. In Paris, Wollstonecraft had seen the guillotine's blade drop incessantly on its victims. The Girondin deputies,[1] as well as Wollstonecraft's friend Madame Roland, were killed while Wollstonecraft was in Paris. In the memoir William Godwin published for Wollstonecraft in 1798,[2] shortly after her death following complications from childbirth, he wrote that Wollstonecraft described her emotions at the "death of Brissot, Vergniaud, and the twenty deputies" as "one of the most intolerable sensations she had ever experienced" (Godwin in Holmes 1987, 244).

Personal circumstances, too, interacted with the political to fuel Wollstonecraft's grief. While in Paris, she met Gilbert Imlay, an

American entrepreneur with whom she had hoped to form the domestic counterpart to revolutionary politics—a "revolutionary conjugality" (Kelly 1996, 170). With Imlay, she experimented with love and commitment outside of marriage and gave birth to a daughter but was dismayed by what she considered the premature end to the relationship. Wollstonecraft's letters to Imlay seem to expose her as the kind of woman she would not have wanted to be. She became a lonely and rejected lover, a single mother without the support and name of a man, and was seen as undeserving of respect in the eyes of society.

Whereas in other work Wollstonecraft shied away from personal revelation, this memoir and her letters reveal her fears and desires. Feminist theorists sometimes include *A Short Residence in Sweden* and *Maria, or the Wrongs of Woman* in their work on Wollstonecraft, yet there is a marked tendency to separate Wollstonecraft's political writings from these more literary works.[3] When the melancholy Wollstonecraft is analyzed alongside Wollstonecraft the feminist theorist, there is an effort to reconcile the two selves rather than to analyze why and how Wollstonecraft could succumb to the version of feminine sensibility she condemned in her political philosophy.[4] I contend that though Wollstonecraft remains respectful of reason and virtue in her letters, her writing represents the continuing conflict she experienced between what we might call feminist authority, or her understanding of herself as writer and thinker, and feminine sensibility, or how she understood herself as a woman struggling with the demands of femininity. In her masterly introduction to Wollstonecraft's collected letters, Janet Todd (2003, x) observes, "At different times the letters reveal her wanting to reconcile different irreconcilables—integrity and sexual longing, the needs and duties of a woman, motherhood and intellectual life, fame and domesticity, reason and passion—but all are marked by similar strenuousness, a wish to be true to the complexity she felt."

Mary Jacobus (1995) ventures that the scholarly tendency to separate these two aspects of Wollstonecraft's work is one index of the tormented relationship modern feminists have with their feminist mother. "As heirs to her [Wollstonecraft's] melancholia as well as to her feminism, we are bound to resist (or fall in love with) her legacy of impossible mourning" (p. 80). As a result of falling in love with this legacy, I am most interested in the dilemmas of the political theorist depicted here as a single mother, an unconventional woman, a rejected lover, and an intrepid woman traveling alone to isolated and sometimes dangerous destinations.[5]

Godwin suggested that when Wollstonecraft met Gilbert Imlay in Paris, she was convinced that he could be the man with whom she might reinvent domestic life. As Gary Kelly (1996, 177) remarked, "At first Imlay seemed the ideal revolutionary man she had called for in *A Vindication of the Rights of Woman*—uncontaminated by court culture, fit for the revolutionary domesticity that was to bring about a revolutionary society." Godwin (1987, 242) commented on the change of Wollstonecraft's character resulting from the "change of fortune" she experienced in her personal life on meeting and falling in love with Gilbert Imlay in France. Having reminded readers of the series of misfortunes Wollstonecraft faced in her short life, including the early death of her mother and her best friend Fanny Blood, Godwin (1987, 242–43) emphasized the hope and renewal Wollstonecraft felt upon her attachment to the American Imlay:

> Mary now reposed herself upon a person, of whose honour and principles she had the most exalted idea. She nourished an individual affection, which

she saw as no necessity of subjecting to restraint; and a heart like hers was not formed to nourish affection by halves. Her conception of Mr. Imlay's "tenderness and worth had twisted him closely round her heart"; and she "indulged the thought, that she had thrown out some tendrils, to cling to the elm by which she wished to be supported." Her confidence was entire, her love was unbounded.

Soon pregnant with Imlay's child, Wollstonecraft saw the Revolution take a dangerous turn. In the winter of 1793–94, daily witness to the "growing cruelties of Robespierre" (Wollstonecraft 1987, 244), Wollstonecraft struggled "to entertain a favorable opinion of human nature" (p. 245). People were being killed by the dozens,[6] prices of all commodities soared out of control, the cold in Paris was intolerable, and firewood was scarce. Wollstonecraft had seen friends, members of the more moderate Girondins, executed, and she was repulsed by the "blood of the guillotine appear[ing] fresh upon the pavement" (Holmes 1987, 244). As Todd (2000, 242) remarked, "it was a dark time to be bearing a child," even more so out of wedlock. Todd also reminded us of Wollstonecraft's limited choices: Though France was far from the ideal environment for a pregnant woman, back at home in England "a woman, fearing the label of whore, would [need to] hide her shame until she might emerge childless" (ibid.).

Shortly after the birth of their daughter, Fanny, who was born in Le Havre in May 1794—the month Robespierre established his Cult of the Supreme Being—Imlay and Wollstonecraft were separated by Imlay's business travels. By the time Wollstonecraft returned to Paris with Fanny, Imlay had sailed for England on business, leaving Wollstonecraft increasingly fearful of his waning interest in her and their daughter. During these months, Wollstonecraft wrote to Imlay constantly, finding his return letters ever colder and more distant. And though Robespierre had fallen, the situation in Paris continued to be politically volatile.

Disappointed both by the Revolution as well as revolutionary conjugality, Wollstonecraft struggled to make sense of her personal life and political events. In February 1795, she wrote to Imlay:

> This has been such a period of barbarity and misery, I ought not to complain of having my share. I wish one moment that I had never heard of the cruelties that have been practiced here, and the next envy the mothers who have been killed with their children. Surely I had suffered enough in life, not to be cursed with a fondness, that burns up the vital stream I am imparting. You will think me mad: I would I were so, that I could forget my misery—so that my head or heart would be still. (Wollstonecraft 1979, 279)

She lamented the fact that her own daughter would grow up to face the tyranny of men:

> I have gotten into a melancholy mood, you perceive. You know my opinion of men in general; you know that I think them systematic tyrants, and that it is the rarest thing in the world to meet with a man with sufficient delicacy of feeling to govern desire. When I am thus sad, I lament that my little darling, fondly as I doat [sic] on her, is a girl....I am sorry to have a tie to a world that for me is ever sown with thorns. (Wollstonecraft 1979, 273)

Wollstonecraft's subsequent trip to Sweden, Norway, and Denmark with one-year-old Fanny in tow was a voyage born of personal distress and political disappointment. "Damped by the tears of disappointed affection," Wollstonecraft traveled in an attempt to forget the "horrors [she] had witnessed in France" (Wollstonecraft 1987, 68). Wollstonecraft undertook the voyage at the urging of Imlay, possibly because he feared for her mental health and wanted to occupy her with travel and business or possibly because he needed her to do his bidding in a shady mercantile adventure in Norway.[7] Indeed, Wollstonecraft also needed money to support herself and her child. Perhaps Imlay wished to distract Wollstonecraft from her "obsession" with him, but he also recognized her ability to carry out a serious and complicated enterprise, no matter what her state of mind. Thus, it was decided that Wollstonecraft would go to Scandinavia "as Imlay's business agent; she would also resume professional work by keeping an account of her trip" to be published on her return (Kelly 1996, 174).

Wollstonecraft's struggle with the demands of femininity is nowhere clearer than in her letters from Sweden. In these letters, Wollstonecraft (1987) presented herself almost simultaneously as a persecuted, suffering woman and a strong, intellectual, and political woman. She was the rejected lover, the single mother, one who suffered the "enthusiasm of her character"; she was also a "woman of observation," a woman who daringly travels alone to parts unknown and unseen, a woman who asks "men's questions" (p. 68). This tension is maintained throughout. Wollstonecraft simultaneously presented herself in her many roles as mother, lover, intellectual, and adventurer:

> What, I exclaimed, is this active principle which keeps me still awake?... Why fly my thoughts abroad when everything around me appears at home? My child was sleeping with equal calmness—innocent and sweet as the closing flowers....Some recollections, attached to the idea of home, mingled with reflections respecting the state of society I had been contemplating that evening, made a tear drop on the rosy cheek I had just kissed; and emotions that trembled on the brink of extacy [sic] and agony gave a poignancy to my sensations, which made me feel more alive than usual. (p. 69)

Wollstonecraft most clearly felt the melancholy and disappointment she had experienced in her life as an intellectual woman when she considered her own daughter's future:

> You know that as a female I am particularly attached to her—I feel more
> than a mother's fondness and anxiety, when I reflect on the dependent and
> oppressed state of her sex. I dread lest she should be forced to sacrifice her
> heart to her principles, or principles to her heart. With trembling hand I
> shall cultivate sensibility, and cherish delicacy of sentiment, lest, whilst I
> lend fresh blushes to the rose, I sharpen the thorns that will wound the
> breast I would fain guard—I dread to unfold her mind, lest it should render
> her unfit for the world she is to inhabit—Hapless woman! what a fate is
> thine! (p. 97)

Given Wollstonecraft's prior work and reputation, her mention of
the intense dilemmas of the thinking woman is most remarkable.
Wollstonecraft lamented that in the world as presently constituted,
a woman must be forced to sacrifice her heart to her principles, or
principles to her heart. Under these terms a woman is, quite unjustly,
forced to choose between feminine sensibility and masculine reason.
Contrary to her prescriptions for the best marriage as based in friendship, detailed in *A Vindication of the Rights of Woman*, Wollstonecraft's
love for Imlay had led her to hope that she could act on sexual passion
and romantic desire while maintaining her own independence as well
as the respect of her male counterpart. The sexual openness of revolutionary Paris—as opposed to the confines of English society—had
led Wollstonecraft to hope for, and to try to enact, a new revolutionary
domesticity with Imlay in the city of a political and social revolution
that was to usher in gender equality. But both attempts had failed.
Her experiment with Imlay ended in betrayal, just as the Revolution
betrayed both liberal principles and promises to women. What routes
for women, especially thinking women, were available now? At another
moment in her travels, Wollstonecraft (1987, 158) envied the image of
domestic bliss she thought she glimpsed watching some strangers.

> It was Saturday, and the evening was uncommonly serene. In the villages I everywhere saw preparations for Sunday; and I passed by a little car loaded with rye, that presented, for the pencil and heart, the sweetest picture of a harvest home I had ever beheld! A little girl was mounted astraddle on a shaggy horse, brandishing a stick over its head; the father was walking at the side of the car with a child in his arms, who must have come to meet him with tottering steps, the little creature stretching out his arms to cling around his neck; and a boy, just above petticoats, was labouring hard, with a fork, behind, to keep the sheaves from falling. My eyes followed them to the cottage, and an involuntary sigh whispered to my heart, that I envied the mother, much as I dislike cooking, who was preparing their pottage. I was returning to my babe, who may never experience a father's care or tenderness. The bosom that nurtured her, heaved with a pang at the thought which only an unhappy mother could feel.

This passage is fascinating not only because it invites us so willingly into the thoughts of one of our most famous feminist mothers but also because of the contradictions and dilemmas it exposes at the surface of this feminist woman's life. Mary Wollstonecraft, keen observer of the domestic and political inequality stemming from the sexual division of labor obscured by romantic idealism, here failed to scratch beneath the surface of the image of domestic bliss. Much as she disliked cooking she still said she envied the mother. As Wollstonecraft presented herself in this passage, she was an abandoned woman, reduced for the moment to taking refuge in romantic illusions.

But this was only for a moment. Though Wollstonecraft (1987, 84) was extraordinarily interested in the common people she met during her travels, she knew she could never live such a simple life, especially that of the common woman: "My heart would frequently be interested; but my mind would languish for more companionable society." Her desires alternated between the seemingly uncomplicated commune with nature, sentiment, and emotion and the need to expand and to explore her intellect. Though the life of the common woman would in some ways constitute an easier path, Wollstonecraft knew that she was and must remain an exceptional woman. Enamored with the simplicity of nature, "romantic views," and "purest air," Wollstonecraft nevertheless situated herself as firmly rooted in "polished circles of the world" (p. 122). Studying Wollstonecraft's writing on portrayals of genius and femininity, Christine Battersby (1989, 95) noted that Wollstonecraft's desire was for a world in which a "woman could combine genius with love." She was willing to give herself room to experience the strongest emotions but also endeavored to curb them within the boundaries of what Wollstonecraft (1987, 122) called her "thinking mind." She claimed that "for years I have endeavored to calm an impetuous tide—labouring to make my feeling take an orderly course" (p. 111). Wollstonecraft was overwhelmed with melancholy, yet she sought to curb her emotions with the powers of reason: "My thoughts fly from the wilderness to the polished circles of the world, till recollecting its vices and follies, I bury myself in the woods, but find it necessary to emerge again, that I may not lose sight of the wisdom and virtue which exalts my nature" (p. 122).

At times Wollstsonecraft (1987, 122) even wondered if she "ought to rejoice at having turned over in this solitude a new page in the history of [her] own heart." She longed to believe again in the plans for the future she had once felt were within her reach: "Phantoms of bliss! Ideal forms of excellence! Again embrace me in your magic circle, and wipe clear from my remembrance the disappointments which render the sympathy painful, which experience rather increases than damps; by giving the indulgence of feeling the sanction of reason" (pp. 128–29). In this moment of unguarded grief, Wollstonecraft wallowed in the multiple disappointments she experienced with her personal and political hopes. Her imagination, which she rooted in emotion and sentiment, let her dare to wish for the equality of women, the success of revolutionary principles, and the possibility of sexual passion and romantic love outside of the bounds of traditional marriage. In both her *Vindications*, Wollstonecraft claimed that reason would guide citizens toward this enlightened future. But in her personal reflections, reason played a different role. Reason saved her from the deepest depths of sorrow, yet it also cast the cold light of temperance on her once wild dreams for a better future.

Staël's Exile

Staël (2000, 3) began her reflections on her exile in the following way: "It is not to draw public attention to myself that I have set out to relate the circumstances of ten years of exile. The misfortunes I have endured, however bitter, count for so little amid the public disasters we confront that it would be shameful to speak of oneself if the events that concern us were not connected to the great cause of endangered humanity." Here Staël boldly claimed that from her experience we might understand something greater about forces that threaten humanity. Linking her intimate personal experiences with Europe's political plight from the start, Staël curiously attempted the seemingly impossible: to "disappear into the background as I tell my own story" (p. 4).

As we saw in chapter 2, unlike Wollstonecraft, Staël put women's feminine identity at the center of her analysis to lay the groundwork for a protofeminist politics based exclusively in feminine sensibility. Though willing to adopt these notions she also, however, transformed them to make a political and public statement. Staël was outspoken in her criticism of the manly citizenship embraced by the Jacobins as well as Napoleon's banishment of women from the public sphere. Thus, though Wollstonecraft's reputation lay in a challenge to feminine sensibility and Staël's in its embrace, both women shared the conviction that domestic and political change must proceed simultaneously.

Mary D. Sheriff (1996, 244) noted, "Known for her conversation, intelligence, and wit, Madame de Staël was in every way an exceptional woman." Avriel Goldberger (Introduction to Staël 2000, xv) observed that Staël "loved politics but had one flaw, and it was fatal: she had been born female at a time when the political theater was closed to women, when they could maneuver only behind the scenes." Napoleon harbored a deep suspicion of all intellectuals, but in 1800 he singled out Staël for persecution after she published *De la littérature* [*On Literature Considered in Relation to Social Institutions*], an Enlightenment and cosmopolitan piece inherently at odds with Napoleon's reactionary goals. Even before the decree of exile, Napoleon saw to it that Staël's work was attacked in the press, subjecting her novel *Delphine* to the same treatment two years later. Staël was shut out of salons, her writing was censored and banned, and former friends—prominent intellectuals and political actors—refused to associate with her as Napoleon placed her in a pariah category.

Like Wollstonecraft's *A Short Residence in Sweden*, Staël's *Ten Years of Exile* is simultaneously a travel memoir, the story of a woman and a man, and an analysis of the myriad ways in which the domestic and the personal serve as a marker for the political. In contrast to Wollstonecraft's memoir, however, Staël placed herself at the center of political events enveloping Europe. After all, the man who disappointed her was not just any lover but rather Napoleon Bonaparte, dictator of the nineteenth century. Staël portrayed Napoleon as an insatiable tyrant and herself as an exceptional woman denied political access. Staël wrote herself as a suffering heroine, but one who suffers due to her enormous influence over the political process. She was interested not only in how Napoleon's actions affected her but also how they index individual, familial, and political tyranny. As France's emperor and military commander, Napoleon was at the center of political turmoil enveloping the continent. Banned from France, Staël fled to Germany, Austria, Poland, and Russia in advance of Napoleon's armies. She was received throughout Europe by political dignitaries and in Russia by Czar Alexander I and Empress Elizabeth. Linda Orr (1992, 129) noted that Staël's "traveling salon (Germany, England, Sweden) could have helped crystallize the opposition that did eventually bring [Napoleon] down."

Thus, while Wollstonecraft's memoir challenged her reputation as immune to the traps and snares of feminine sensibility, Staël's work revealed her to be much more than a champion of feminine sensibility. Here in Staël's *Ten Years*, we uncover a remarkably strong woman, challenger to Napoleon, hidden behind the screen of the suffering heroine. Each memoir shows the woman political theorist to be much more complex than she initially seemed.

Throughout *Ten Years*, Staël (2000) insisted on probing the personal and the domestic to judge the health of the political. Only through attention to individual and personal experience, Staël claimed, can we understand the fate of the whole of humanity. Though "limited," her perspective drew attention to the "vast picture" (p. 4). Reading *Ten Years of Exile* we discover Staël's certainty that her own situation as a "defenseless, persecuted woman" (p. 30) speaks volumes about the immorality of Napoleon's politics. She identified as—or with—suffering heroines as one way to shed light on the tyrannical political forces that crush particular individuals. As we saw in chapter 2, Staël identified with the excluded and vilified, even the infamous Marie-Antoinette. The queen's execution was, in Staël's analysis, an indication that revolutionary forces had run amok. Staël called attention to Marie-Antoinette's role as a mother and as a suffering heroine. As discussed in chapter 2, Staël argued that the queen's execution revealed the Revolution's wish to silence women who dared to be political, even as they attempted to conform to the feminine role. The queen was clearly a political woman, but she was also a mother, a wife, and a woman in a foreign country. Throughout each stage of the Revolution, Staël spoke against ideological excess. Her political loyalties shifted to accommodate her humanitarian commitments and her concern for the individual. When being a woman became construed as membership in a pariah category during the Jacobin and into the Napoleonic era, Staël's sympathies turned toward her excluded sisters, and her focus on gender issues sharpened.

Ironically, Staël hoped to gain favor with Napoleon when he first came to power in 1799. As an outspoken defender of women's and individual rights, Staël craved influence on the First Consul in these matters. Staël had been disillusioned by the Revolution's turn toward Terror and particularly outraged by the Jacobin's emphasis on a manly citizenship and exclusion of women from politics. Early on in her memoir Staël (2000, 29) noted that many people in France thought Bonaparte had not done anything "precisely culpable as yet; many people insisted that he would protect France from great woes." Indeed,

Staël admitted, "In fact, if just then he had sent me word that he would be reconciled with me, I would have been overjoyed if anything" (ibid.). When Bonaparte first came to power he had not yet formulated a "plan for universal monarchy," but after 18 Brumaire, his system was to "infringe on the liberty of France and the independence of Europe every day" (p. 34). And though she desired political involvement, she was unwilling to play politics according to Napoleon's rules. But he was "never willing to make peace with anyone without exacting something contemptible in exchange" (pp. 29–30). "He knew that I was attached to my friends, to France, to my works, to my tastes, to society; in taking from me everything that made up my happiness, he meant to unsettle me enough to write some platitude in the hope of its winning my return" (p. 113). Staël was never willing to submit, but she paid dearly for her principles: "Society withdrew from you along with the government's favor, an unbearable situation—especially for a woman—and whose cuts and stabs no one can know without having experienced it" (p. 29).

She took on the role of suffering heroine, then, not only as a way to draw attention to her own situation but also to connect her experience to the greater dangers of political tyranny. Though she had hoped to influence the dictator, she feared his resistance to intellectual women early on. Yet Staël not only was willing to speak her mind; she also continued to publish. Napoleon found this an especially repulsive quality in a woman. Chased across the globe, denied her political and social life in Paris amid friends and political colleagues, Staël (2000, 105) likened her forced exile to an "imprisonment more terrible than death."

> You will be astonished, perhaps, that I compare exile to death, but
> Bolingbroke himself argues which of the two penalties is more cruel. Cicero,

> who managed to brave proscription, could not endure exile. One comes
> upon more men who are courageous in the face of the scaffold than of the
> loss of their native land. In all codes of law, perpetual banishment is con-
> sidered punishment for a capital crime, and in France the whim of one man
> nonchalantly inflicts what conscientious judges only reluctantly impose on
> criminals. (p. 72)

Staël openly criticized Napoleon for his inability to feel empathy for
his victims, his dismissal of his critics, and his unquenchable thirst
for power. Staël lamented that France had to constantly hear of the
"victories of a man whose every success has been at the expense of all"
(p. 37). His "great talent is for terrifying the weak and making use of
immoral men" (p. 38). She continued, "If tyranny had only the direct
support of its partisans, it would never last; the astonishing thing,
and one that shows human wretchedness above all else, is that most
mediocre men serve the event. They do not have the strength to think
beyond an accomplished fact, and when an oppressor has triumphed,
when a victim is ruined, they hasten to justify, not precisely the tyrant,
but the destiny that has made him its instrument" (pp. 145–46).

This insight could be characterized as quintessentially Staël. As her
volumes on the French Revolution and her novels aptly demonstrate,
Staël abhorred uncritical acceptance of any status quo. But she paid
dearly for her identity as an exceptional woman willing to publicly
voice her criticism. Staël (2000, 117) observed that the persecution of
women is all the more barbaric as "their nature is at once sensitive and
weak; they suffer afflictions more acutely and are less capable of the
strength needed to break free of them" (Staël 2000, 117). Julia Kristeva
(1995, 169) comments, "Although a woman of letters contributes to
the dignity of the arts in the same way that men do, she is more sus-
ceptible to the adversity of glory than a man would be."

While it is one thing to express an opinion as a woman in the salon, which might be considered harmless, even charming, it is another thing completely to write and publish about political events. Both Wollstonecraft and Staël were guilty of this crime. Like Wollstonecraft, who sought to challenge domestic and political conventions concerning women, Staël was an extraordinary woman who defied personal and political norms for women and claimed public attention due to her intellect. Because of this—and like Wollstonecraft—she suffered. Staël (2000) wrote of her intense fear of isolation, of concern for her family, and of the guilt of endangering her friends and taking her children away from the life they knew.

> They never stopped telling me that my whole life was to be spent within the two leagues separating Coppet from Geneva. If I stayed, I would need to part with my sons, who were of an age to seek a career; I would impose the most forlorn prospects on my daughter by having her share my fate....It was all over for my talent, for my happiness, for my existence, since it is dreadful to be of no use to one's children and to harm one's friends. (p. 118)

Here Staël recalled her difficult decision: "one of the most considerable that might be encountered in a woman's private life" (p. 119). In 1812 she fled from Coppet to an unknown destination, leaving behind a fourteen-year-old son and taking a younger son and daughter to an uncertain future. But once again, Staël reflected on her own personal torment and her fate as a woman intellectual as a way to think about the larger looming political dangers.

> No deputy will express his thought freely, no writer will dare express himself any longer if he can be banished when his candor displeases. No man will dare speak sincerely if it can cost the happiness of his entire family. A woman, above all, meant to support and reward enthusiasm, will strive to smother her generous feelings if they must result either in her being taken

from the objects of her affection, or in seeing her loved ones sacrifice their lives to follow her into exile. (p. 73)

Staël argued that because she "suffered cruelly," she was in a unique position to point out "all that must lead to never allowing a sovereign the right of arbitrary exile" (ibid.). She claimed that her own suffering led to better insight and to an ability to express the empathy and emotion absent from revolutionary as well as Napoleonic France. Staël's exile opened her eyes and ears to the "immense intellectual treasures outside of France" (p. 75) in Germany, Russia, and Sweden, moving her also to think about the value of individual liberty, the danger of public opinion, and the tyranny one man can exert over an entire continent.

Staël wrote herself as a persecuted heroine precisely so that we, as readers, will empathize with her. She wrote herself as the suffering heroine much like her own literary characters, Delphine and Corinne, who suffer due to their status and behavior as exceptional women. She styled herself in these memoirs as a curious combination of the persecuted and the uncommonly gifted woman. As Madelyn Gutwirth remarked, "Staël speaks to the still unresolved conundrum of women's aspirations. Fictions from her pen plot the degree of entrapment of will and heart subduing women's powers. Her own 'foreignness' to the political, social, and personal order in which she found herself forced her to traverse geographic frontiers, at first unwillingly, finally triumphantly" (Gutwirth, Goldberger, and Szmurlo 1991, xi).

She was, as her memoir indicates, a woman highly unlike other women of her day. Staël's remarkable ability to make herself heard and to express her opinions according to her own conscience could be what made her seem such a threat to Napoleon. Staël displayed the quali-

ties of an emotional woman who sought to extend and to mold that sensibility to guide reason and intellect. Despite her personal anguish and the grief her notoriety produced, Staël (2000) never regretted the choice to live her life as an intellectual, political woman. At the beginning of her memoir, she acknowledged the act of writing as a way to express her intellect and even to save her life.

> But even though this last piece of writing [*On Germany*] won me bitter persecution, literature still seems to me no less a source of enjoyment and regard, even for a woman. I attribute what I have suffered in life to the circumstances that, from the moment I entered society, associated me with the interests of liberty upheld by my father and my friends, but the form of talent that made me known as a writer has always brought me more pleasure than pain...In a word, even if one must suffer injustice for a long time, I cannot conceive of a better shelter from it than meditation on philosophy and the emotion prompted by eloquence. These faculties put at our disposal a whole world of discoveries and feelings where we always breathe freely. (p. 35)

This statement, in the context of her life and life's writing, expresses the dilemmas historically faced by intellectual women with a feminist consciousness. Simone de Beauvoir noted that independent women are an aberration from the feminine norm and are almost always considered monstrous creatures. Throughout *The Second Sex*, Beauvoir often cited Staël as an example of the independent woman, classed as one willing to battle with powerful men and to express her own desires as a knowing subject. Staël's eagerness to challenge Napoleon's politics—her unwillingness to bend to his desires—marks *Ten Years of Exile* as a reflection on revolutions, both personal and political. Staël's account of her exile clearly reveals her identity as a woman who is bound by both feminine sensibility, including emotional responsibilities and commitments to family and friends, as well as feminist authority. Most dangerously, for the eyes of society, Staël was politically engaged, always willing to take risks and endure hardships for the "cause of liberty."

Dilemmas of Love and Revolution

Authorship is a heavy weight for female shoulders especially in the sunshine of prosperity.

Mary Wollstonecraft, *Letter to Everina*
Wollstonecraft from Paris, 1792 (Wardle 1979, 209)

Braving public opinion is an extremely dangerous course for women to take; it is necessary, in order to dare to do such a thing, that they make themselves feel—to use a poetic comparison—*a tripled band of brass around the heart.*

Germaine de Staël, *Delphine*, 1802 (1995, 116)

As revealed in their travel memoirs, Wollstonecraft and Staël come across as decidedly more complex—and possibly more problematic for certain kinds of feminist interpretation—than prior work has revealed. Wollstonecraft is not simply the feminist theorist but is also a woman who longs for love, albeit in a new form of intimacy transformed by the revolutionary process. Hoping to revolutionize domesticity and politics simultaneously, which was argued as an inherently integrated project in the 1792 *Vindication of the Rights of Woman*, by 1795 Wollstonecraft was deeply disappointed with progress toward each goal. In her personal letters written from Paris, as well as the *Letters from Sweden*, Wollstonecraft seemed to see political revolution as well as potential transformation in ideals of domesticity as both deeply paradoxical. Revolution was both a movement toward human perfectibility and monstrous terror; romantic love outside of marriage

contained the possibility for infinite transformation but also unfathomable depth of loss and sorrow.

Smith (1996, 1063) places Staël in the company of the "mad, drugged-out world of the geniuses, in the pulsating romantic climate of sensual, embodied knowledge." This description is accurate, but it only presents part of the story. Staël was both an excessive, narcissistic Romantic heroine and Napoleon's powerful rival. To fully understand Staël's legacy we must remember that she always retained her status as a vitally powerful political woman, albeit one quite disillusioned by history's patterns during her lifetime. Staël's disillusionment takes center political stage when she, a woman recognized as both exceptional and political, was denied political access and was exiled from France. Staël's suffering at the order of Napoleon was brought on solely by her identity as a political woman who opposed Napoleon's tyranny. Staël witnessed the disappointments of the Revolution and then, living much longer than Wollstonecraft, also saw the Napoleonic Civil Codes become law in 1804. Under the Napoleonic Codes, wives were subject to their husbands; had no rights in the administration of common property; were forbidden to give, sell, or mortgage property; and could acquire property only with written consent of their husbands. Napoleon imposed his own view that "women must be treated as irresponsible minors throughout their lives" (Herold 1963, 148) on all of French society. As the daughter of a deposed minister who championed the cause of liberty, Staël saw herself as the "rightful daughter of the Revolution" (Orr 1992, 121-29). Orr explains (ibid.) that Staël's version of history shows a refusal "to separate out her own family romance from her analytic reflections....Daughter of the revolution, daughter of liberty, Madame de Staël was, like the 'true' revolution, exiled wherever she went." Staël analyzed this persecution as both personal and political, based in the gender inequity solidified through the work of a tyrant enacting civil codes absolutely banning women from public life.

Clearly, these two women were not invulnerable to suffering. Indeed, these memoirs suggest that until society undergoes fundamental change in expanding meanings for what being a woman might signify, intellectual, and especially feminist, women might be the most persecuted and unhappy members of the second sex. As public, independent, intellectual women, Wollstonecraft and Staël experienced the fear and fascination associated with their difference from the norm. Smith (1996, 1061) observes that female exceptionality, or genius, makes for a variety of "emotional responses, including anger and confusion." Wollstonecraft and Staël experienced this in struggling with the demands of femininity as well as with what they thought of as their own desires as women. These struggles continue and manifest themselves in the ways women intellectuals are perceived and represented. Smith notes, for example, the tendency in biographical and historical studies "to present the portrait of a hero whose unified character has been purged of contradictory or confusing material" (p. 1059). I contend that without the contradictory and confusing material we will never comprehend the dilemmas our feminist predecessors faced in fighting to be recognized as intellectual women while struggling with the demands of femininity, both materially and existentially.

The melancholy tone of both memoirs documents personal and intellectual survival as well as the necessity of political change. Here we witness the constant struggle between political–public aspiration and personal fulfillment that exacts an enormous price for both women. Though they were never promised a world where women would have it all, the early euphoria of the French Revolution broadened the vision and encouraged the hopes of these political women, for themselves as individuals and for women as a whole. These travel memoirs provide a space and a method of writing the personal allowing each woman to think through personal and political hopes and disappointments. Most revealing in these memoirs are the myriad ways their personal destinies were tied to the failure of political goals.

5. A Feminist Search for Love

Emma Goldman on the Politics of Marriage,
Love, Sexuality, and the Feminine

Emma Goldman is far better known for her dramatic life and for her anarchism than for any contribution to political and feminist theory. An anarchist activist who constantly challenged the political and social status quo, Goldman was a rousing orator, a prolific pamphleteer, as well as founder and editor of the anarchist journal *Mother Earth.* She was jailed many times—once for two years—for her political activity that included support for the labor movement and striking workers, opposition to the WWI draft, advocating free speech and free love, work on the birth control campaign, and opposition to state and government power. In late 1919, Goldman was deported from the United States to the Soviet Union along with several hundred other immigrant radicals including her longtime colleague, friend, and early lover, Alexander Berkman.[1] Hoping to find some of their ideals enacted in the Soviet Revolution,[2] Goldman and Berkman were severely disappointed by the concentration of state power and the suppression of dissidents in their country of birth.[3]

Goldman famously chronicled her anarchist activities in her two-volume autobiography, *Living My Life*. Her presentation is fascinating for its historical context as well as for details of the sacrifices and commitments such an intense political life required. I argue that it is not solely Goldman's political life that makes her important for us to study today. It is in the intersection of her life with her thought—specifically her intimate and sexual life as studied in conjunction with her essays on marriage, sex, love, women's emancipation, and femininity—where a study of Goldman contributes important insights to contemporary feminist debates. Most importantly, she helps us to think about the connections and tensions among sexuality, love, and feminist politics. Chronicled in Goldman's many public speeches and political writings, we witness her philosophical commitment to an anarchist feminism that rejects marriage and the conventional nuclear family. In conjunction with this philosophy, Goldman lived a life of free and open sexual expression and engaged in direct action on behalf of campaigns for birth control, free speech, and complete acceptance of unconventional sexual practices. At the same time, she neither rejected nor condemned romantic love; she placed intimate connections with others as central to her life and her politics, and she suggested that the basis for women's emancipation should spring from the full and complete expression of what she called the feminine instinct.

Rather than turn to the state to deliver women's emancipation, as her sister suffragists were doing, Goldman desired for women to free themselves by unleashing their instincts. She even called for the freedom of "feminine desire" to permit the "deep emotion of the true woman" (Goldman 1969e, 217). This language sounds suspiciously conservative and even echoed some of the language of the antisuffragists. Despite her early and open defense of homosexuality,[4] for example, some of her rhetoric evoking notions of femininity and true womanhood could today be suspected of harboring heterosexist norms and gender essentialism. I argue, however, that Goldman's assumptions about women's difference as well as her vision of sexual freedom and revolutionary love offer a radical critique of intimacy that can contribute to contemporary feminist debates. Since Goldman had to constantly butt up against conventional norms, she was unable to fully express feminine desire in the way she thought would be most freeing. In short, for a variety of reasons Goldman was not always able to live out her beliefs and commitments in the ways she had hoped. Feminists have expressed disappointment over this apparent failure to live up to her ideals, but I take a different approach. An appreciation of Goldman's thought, as well as the interactions of her thought with the social and political climate in which she lived engender multiple historical insights into our own concerns.[5]

Understanding the complexities of Goldman's theory of love and sexuality in conjunction with the dilemmas of desire she experienced in her own life helps us to appreciate not only Goldman's life and work but also the context in which it developed. What might we learn from Goldman's experience about the relationships between theory and practice, one's life and one's beliefs, desires as they conflict with prevailing norms, and how to carry on in the face of disillusionment and despair? I am particularly interested in thinking through Goldman's life and work, as she experienced and understood it, as an example of how even the most radical and forward-thinking women can get trapped by contemporary patriarchal norms under which they live; they often may even unconsciously internalize these norms.

Though Emma Goldman consistently and fundamentally challenged the political status quo, gender roles, and normative sexuality, she remained ambivalent about the meanings attached to femininity. At the same time, Goldman's vision of intimacy and eroticism has plenty to teach us about shortcomings in our contemporary understandings of intimacy, both in what is possible and what is hoped for. I explore Goldman's views on these matters, as well as her writings on her personal experiences, to illuminate continuing paradoxes feminists face in regard to definitions and experiences of femininity.

Goldman's Writings on Marriage, Love, and Sexuality

Goldman (1969a, 62) defined anarchism in the following way:

> [Anarchism] stands for the liberation of the human mind from the dominion of religion; the liberation of the human body from the dominion of property; liberation from the shackles and restraint of government. Anarchism stands for a social order based on the free grouping of individuals for the purpose of producing real social wealth; an order that will guarantee to every human being free access to the earth and full enjoyment of the necessities of life, according to individual desires, tastes, and inclinations.

Goldman's "beautiful ideal" necessitated the emancipation of women. Though many anarchist writers acknowledged the importance of women in the movement, none of the principal male theoreticians gave sustained attention to questions of feminism (Ackelsberg 1991, 17). Like socialist feminist Alexandra Kollantai, Goldman had to fight her political colleagues on the question of which issues were to be labeled "digressions" and which were central to the revolutionary movement. Goldman (1970b, 253) recalled a conversation with Peter Kropotkin, for example, in which he complained that the anarchist paper, *Free*

Society, would do better were it not to "waste so much space discussing sex." And even when there was agreement on the political importance of sexuality, there was, as Ackelsberg (1991, 26) put it, "more than one way to apply an anti-authoritarian analysis to sexual and familial relations." Could free sexual expression exist between equals, and how would women's reproductive role influence her social and political contributions? Goldman was certain about at least one thing. Her life experience had made it clear that no true freedom for women could exist without a fundamental revolution at the intimate level between human beings in their relationships of love and sexuality. She insisted on bringing to light the inequality manifested in our most intimate relationships such as marriage and the nuclear family. Debating the role of women in the 1935 Spanish anarchist movement, Goldman (1975) berated a colleague for claiming it is the "innermost wish" of Spanish women to have "broods of children." Goldman retorted:

> All your assurance not withstanding, I wish to say that I have yet to meet the woman who wants to have many children. That doesn't mean that I ever for a moment denied the fact that most women want to have a *child*, though that, too, has been exaggerated by the male....I have seen too many tragedies in the relations between the sexes; I have seen too many broken bodies and maimed spirits from the sex slavery of woman not to feel the matter deeply or to express my indignation against the attitude of most of you gentlemen. (p. 186)

Goldman recognized sexual and reproductive freedoms as the cornerstone to basic human rights, seeing the curtailment of these freedoms in the most common and accepted practices mandated and promulgated by and through the state. Marriage, for example, condemns women to "life-long dependency, to parasitism, to complete uselessness, individual as well as social" (Goldman 1969c, 228). It compounds the degrading effects of capitalism, annihilating woman's "social consciousness, paralyz[ing] her imagination, and then impos[ing] its gracious protection, which is in reality a snare, a travesty on human character" (p. 235). The home, "though not so large a prison as the factory, has more solid doors and bars" (p. 233).

Ironically and tragically, these prison bars of marriage rarely fail to tantalize young women. The bars appear "golden," their shininess "blind[ing] woman to the price she would have to pay as wife, mother, and housekeeper" (Goldman 1969e, 224). In spite of her oppression, "woman clings tenaciously to the home, to the power that holds her in bondage" (Goldman 1969f, 197). Goldman seized on the heart of the problem: What women are taught to desire also denies them their freedom. The very substance of what makes a woman feminine is what holds her in bondage. Being a mother, a wife, and a lover, as defined by Goldman's historical moment, was to be financially, emotionally, socially, and politically dependent. Studying sexuality in nineteenth-century feminist thought, feminist historians Ellen DuBois and Linda Gordon (1983, 12) noted the contradictions women lived: "What was conceived as women's greatest virtue, their passionate and self-sacrificing commitment to their children, their capacity for love itself, was a leading factor in their victimization."

But the options for women were very limited. A woman might even be aware of her potential slavery within marriage yet walk into it open-eyed having surveyed other, even less desirable alternatives. "We find many emancipated women who prefer marriage, with all its deficiencies, to the narrowness of an unmarried life, narrow and unendurable because of the chains of moral and social prejudice that cramp and bind her nature" (Goldman 1969e, 221).

What were the alternatives beyond marriage? If a woman were to remain unmarried, she might be labeled a spinster, a loose woman, or a whore. Partially in response to these limited alternatives, the late nineteenth century witnessed the rise of the feminist movement. Women activists of many political persuasions advanced new visions of gender relations, women's social role, and even, of course, women's potential role in politics. Some feminist historians have called the late nineteenth century a "golden age for single women," noting opportunities for gainful employment, and even new fashions—out with confining corsets and hoopskirts, replaced by dark skirts and simple blouses (Ware 2002, 3). Yet even the more progressive options had their drawbacks. Goldman claimed (1969e) at the time that taking on the role of the new woman was to accept the notion that women must make themselves professional—even male—to be taken seriously. She found that the American suffragists, for example, bought into the idea that if woman is to be emancipated, she must give up on her femininity, her sexuality, and everything that makes her a woman. Echoing conservative antisuffragists but from a profoundly different political perspective, Goldman argued that the suffrage model taught women they needed to relinquish any claims to femininity to be free.

Susan B. Anthony, as the most famous example, seemed to embody this sacrifice of femininity for the cause by being openly critical of the time and effort that "baby-making" stole from the women's rights movement (Wheeler 1995, 49). Goldman argued that the suffrage model made it appear that gaining freedom as a woman could only be purchased at the price of losing one's femininity. And as suffrage became married to the Progressive movement, the emphasis on female morality repulsed Goldman.

Yet though Goldman ridiculed the claim that women were morally superior to men and especially the suffrage claim that "women's nature suited them to the new social responsibilities of the state" (Evans 1997, 154), she also emphasized that women should be allowed and encouraged to freely express what she called their true femininity. Goldman (1969e, 214, 215) clamed that what she identified as partial or external emancipation makes modern woman an "artificial being"—a woman who must be confronted "with the necessity of emancipating herself from emancipation." This woman is a "compulsory vestal, before whom life, with its great clarifying sorrows and its deep, entrancing joys, rolls on without touching or gripping her soul" (p. 217). This woman is not "brave enough to acknowledge that the voice of love is calling, wildly beating against [her] breast, demanding to be heard, to be satisfied" (p. 222). "Emancipation, as understood by the majority of its adherents and exponents, is of too narrow a scope to permit the boundless love and ecstasy contained in the deep emotion of the true woman, sweetheart, mother in freedom" (p. 217).

In short, Goldman disagreed with her suffragist sisters on almost everything. She argued especially vehemently that the fight for, and even the winning of, the vote was bound to ensnare women in new chains.[6] The kind of freedom gained through the law would only constitute a partial freedom, an empty promise. Goldman (1969e, 224) repeatedly insisted that the vote would never and could never fundamentally transform women's lives: A woman might consider herself free but, in reality, she would only be trapped within new confines.

The alternatives, then, as Goldman assessed them, were severely limited. Why would any woman willingly choose to live an unconventional life? Were there even any models women could choose to follow if they desired something more than a conventional life or partial emancipation? Seeking to articulate a vision of true freedom, Goldman offered her own life as an example to others. It is in her life as example that she attempts to most clearly distinguish her politics from the suffragists as well as the moralists inside and outside the suffrage movement. In her two-volume autobiography, *Living My Life*, Goldman spoke candidly about her early and varied sexual experiences, her longings and desires, and her many passionate love affairs, often with younger men.

Throughout her essays on sexuality, love, and marriage, Goldman (1969c) maintained a distinction between marriage and "real love," forced motherhood and the "mother instinct," false/partial and "true" emancipation. "Marriage and love have nothing in common," she wrote (p. 227). A "healthy, grown woman, full of life and passion" must be "free and big enough to learn the mystery of sex without the sanction of State or Church" rather than "subdue her most intense craving, undermine her health, and break her spirit" in the battle to abstain from "the sex experience until a 'good' man comes along to take her unto himself as a wife" (p. 231). Marriage sanctions a motherhood "conceived in hatred, in compulsion" (p. 236): "Yet, if motherhood be of free choice, of love, of ecstasy, of defiant passion," it would be a "free motherhood" (pp. 236, 237).

Real or true freedom, in Goldman's (1969f) definition, does not spring from externally granted laws or rights but rather from woman's soul. If woman is to be truly free, not only in law but in terms of personal liberation, "her development, her freedom, her independence, must come from and through herself" (p. 211). By refusing to be a "sex commodity," refusing to "bear children, unless she wants them," refusing to be "a servant to God, the State, society, the husband, the family," woman will make herself a force for "real love, for peace, for harmony" (ibid.).

But the choice for true freedom involves difficult sacrifices and brings on complicated dilemmas. Can sexual varietism satisfy a person's emotional desires, especially if one has a desire for an intimate confidante and committed lover? Does one have to completely give up on emotional commitment or mutual dependency to be truly free? Goldman's wish was to live her life as a free woman while simultaneously living within community and within mutually supportive bonds. She hoped to live in accordance with her philosophical and political ideals demonstrating that women's lives could be free as well as emotionally satisfying. Goldman (1969e, 224) proclaimed, "If partial emancipation is to become a complete and true emancipation of woman, it will have to do away with the ridiculous notion that to be loved, to be sweetheart and mother, is synonymous with being slave and subordinate."

In an effort to realize the goal of free motherhood and to work toward true emancipation for women, Goldman employed various political methods. She worked tirelessly on the birth control campaign for over ten years. Advocating knowledge of and access to birth control for all women fruitfully combined Goldman's philosophy of anarchist freedom with concrete measures toward political and social change. At the same time, however, the philosophical problem that the reality of children and lovers posed remained a thorny one for anarchist feminists like Goldman. Even if motherhood and mutual reciprocity were freely chosen, could a woman be fully free as an individual when her life was emotionally intertwined with another or, as in motherhood, if she were completely or even partially responsible for another human life? Questions of mutual dependency and reciprocity remained nagging ones for Goldman in her philosophy and in her life.

Living within the Confines of Femininity

Goldman's reading of Mary Wollstonecraft's life points to how she thought about the dilemmas within her own life and the feminist politics of her time. Building her case against the suffragists, Goldman (1981, 116) looked to Wollstonecraft's life to prove the "inadequacy of mere external gain as a means of freeing their [our] sex." Goldman noted,

> Mary's own tragic life proves that economic and social rights for women alone are not enough to fill her life, nor yet enough to fill any deep life, man or woman. It is not true that the deep and fine man—I do not mean the mere male—differs very largely from the deep and fine woman. He too seeks for beauty and love, for harmony and understanding. Mary realized that, because she did not limit herself to her own sex, she demanded freedom for the whole human race. (ibid.)

Referring repeatedly to beauty, love, deep emotion, and affection in this essay on Wollstonecraft, Goldman emphasized the importance of the transformation needed in intimate relations for the revolutionary movement. Goldman identified Wollstonecraft as a kindred spirit, a woman with deep and unwavering commitment to intellectual life and the revolutionary movement. She also identified with her as a woman who longed for true love. As Goldman put it, "Life without love for a character like Mary is inconceivable, and it was her search and yearning for love which hurled her against the rock of inconsistency and despair" (p. 119).

The dilemma of the political and feminist woman in love, the relationship between feminine desire and anarchist feminist authority increasingly occupied Goldman's thoughts as she ended one failing or unsatisfying relationship after another. Goldman's autobiography made clear her frustration in trying to live in intimacy with someone while maintaining her political activities and identity. Her constant desire was to find a partner with whom she could combine politics with intimacy. Ed Brady, for example, an anarchist colleague with whom Goldman shared her life, work, and bed for almost five years, initially was someone on whom Goldman pinned her "dream of love and true companionship" (Goldman 1970b, 151). "Surely it must be possible," she hoped, "for a man and a woman to have a beautiful love life and yet be devoted to a great cause" (p. 154). The tug of war between the emotional and the political was a constant dynamic in Goldman's life: "To the end of my days I should be torn between the yearning for a personal life and the need to giving all to my ideal" (p. 153). Though Goldman claimed that her "giving to humanity" only increased her own need, making her "love and want Ed more" (p. 193), Brady felt, in contrast, that Goldman's "interest in the movement" was nothing but "vanity, nothing but craving for applause and glory and the limelight" (p. 183).

Examining her work in conjunction with her life, it is clear that Goldman was trying to reconcile sexual and individual freedom with the demands of love and mutual reciprocity. Candace Falk (1990), one of Goldman's feminist biographers, argued that the tension between a desire for love and the commitment to anarchist principles remained a primary one throughout Goldman's life. In reading Goldman's enormous volume of correspondence, Falk identified a "tone of desperation, even of resignation" (p. xii) that is unassociated with Emma, the free-dom fighter. When Goldman "was vulnerable to political repression, she responded with daring and defiance, but when she was vulnerable in a love relationship it triggered feelings of abandonment and des-peration" (p. xiv).

Goldman's dream of ongoing political partnership and intimacy was only realized for moments at a time. When she met another of her lovers, Ben Reitman, Goldman (1970b, 425) hoped it might signal the start of a "new chapter in [her] life" with someone "who was lover, companion, and manager." Reitman was Goldman's lover during her most tumultuous years on the birth control campaign. Goldman wrote of the "great hunger for someone who would love the woman in me and yet who would also be able to share my work" (p. 433). In *Living My Life*, Goldman intentionally denied her intense passion for Reitman and the ways she was beholden to her desire to make the relationship work.[7] In a 1909 letter to Reitman, she expressed the con-tradictions she felt in her life. Goldman (2001, 98) desperately feared losing Reitman's love and companionship while still desiring to be a model of freedom and independence for others:

> Meetings, free speech, are nothing to me now, if my love, my life, my peace, my very soul is to be mutilated. Work with you, so long as I had faith in your love, meant the greatest, sweetest joy in life. That may account for my utter abandonment, my utter dissolution to my love for you. That may also account, why I the woman who has been treated with respect by friend and foe, could crouch on her knees and beg and plead with you…I have no right to bring a message to people when there is no message in my soul. I have no right to speak of freedom when I myself have become abject slave in my love.

Goldman despised her dependency—on Brady, on Reitman, and on her own longing for intimacy and affection from another human being. Living outside the boundaries of conventional society and defying all expectations for women made it nearly insurmountable for Goldman to achieve the kind of emotional fulfillment for which she so desperately hoped. This was certainly not an unusual situation for feminists of the period, particularly for anarchist feminists as they chose to so radically reject social norms. Feminist theorist Ann Ferguson (1995, 373) reminds us that "our fragmented subjectivities require support by a number of oppositional communities that provide alternative meanings and material support." Though Goldman was the center of multiple anarchist communities and alternative forms of family, she continued to long for a special intimacy with one individual. Redefining models of family and ways of intimacy was a particularly difficult challenge for women of Goldman's historical moment. Others, too, were struggling with these same questions, yet lacking the material and psychological resources it would take to so radically redefine ways of loving, each individual felt they were struggling alone. Documenting "modern love" in Greenwich Village in the early twentieth century, Ellen Kay Trimberger (1983, 143) argued, "Women might give each other private support, but there was not at this time a women's movement that publicly discussed changes in personal life, marriage, and sex, nor one that helped women articulate what changes were in their interests."

Goldman's contemporary, feminist Voltairine de Cleyre, also struggled alone with questions of self-definition. In a study of anarchist women, Margaret Marsh (1981, 135) argued that de Cleyre's correspondence reveals "that grinding poverty drove her to contemplate marriage for economic security, that she suffered periods of acute despondency because she considered her life a failure, and that on one occasion her depression nearly resulted in suicide." Goldman (1975, 128), remarking to Berkman in one letter that she longed to express "love and affection for some human being of [her] own," suggested a break with the philosophy of anarchist feminists who argue that sexual freedom necessarily implies a rejection of emotional possession. Putting sexual freedom and the critique of domesticity at the center of her analyses, de Cleyre felt that to conquer jealousy and to reject any claims or hold over any other individual was central to a revolutionary strategy. To be jealous or possessive was to make a claim to private property.[8] Though Goldman (1998, 215) made similar claims against jealousy, seeing it as the "most prevalent evil of our mutilated love life," she tempered her condemnation by acknowledging that the "two worlds" of "two human beings, of different temperament, feelings, and emotions" must meet in "freedom and equality" if they are to conquer the "green-eyed monster" (pp. 221, 216, respectively).

As Goldman fluctuated between desires for political and personal fulfillment, times of political disappointment became for her the moments when she felt most powerfully that something was lacking in her life as a woman. Writing to Berkman in 1925 of an anarchist friend and colleague, Goldman (1975) described the "tragedy of all us modern women":

> It is a fact that we are removed only by a very short period from our traditions, the traditions of being loved, cared for, protected, secured, and above all, the time when women could look forward to an old age of children, a home and someone to brighten their lives. Being away from all that by a mere fraction of time, most modern women, especially when they see age growing upon them, and if they have given out of themselves so abundantly, begin to feel the utter emptiness of their existence, the lack of the *man*, whom they love and who loves them, the comradeship and companionship that grows out of such a relation, the home, a child. And above all the

> economic security either through the man or their own definite independent efforts. Nearly every modern woman I have known and have read about has come to [this] condition. (p. 131)

This is a condition Goldman knows well. Despite the fact that she struggled to free herself from the confines of traditional marriage and motherhood, despite the fact that she lived a life of sexual freedom and political activity, in private correspondence Goldman said that she suffered from having failed to achieve a long-term relationship that would satisfy her feminine desire.

Goldman's "Beautiful Ideal"

How might we understand the meanings and contradictions of what Goldman refers to as feminine desire? When Goldman made reference to *femininity,* the *mother instinct,* and *woman's soul,* she articulated a very basic difference between men and women, but she intentionally did not specify whether that difference is based in biology, psychology, social–political hierarchies, psycholinguistic–symbolic organization, or some combination of these factors. Goldman's appeals to difference were often used rhetorically but reflect her own observations about her life and the lives of other women she knew. Goldman's radical life and practical activities put her in contact and solidarity with huge numbers of women of all classes and types. In her lectures and campaigns for birth control and women's sexual freedom, she reached out to women of the middle classes; at the same time, working for the rights of prostitutes and gays, Goldman appealed to both lower and middle classes and radical and liberal audiences. In addition, her years working as a midwife for impoverished women who could not afford doctors, health care, or a back-alley abortion put Goldman in intimate contact with the destitution of the poorest and most desperate women.

Yet in spite of Goldman's knowledge of the ways women are divided, she still often grouped women together in a category without any subtle or even obvious distinctions. As a propagandist, Goldman tended to exaggerate many of her claims, speaking of women in an uncomplicated, even essentialist, way. While fully aware of the differences between and among women, Goldman still found it appropriate to speak of women as differentiated as a group within a structure of gender inequity. And she continued to speak of feminine desire.

In challenging the notion of a rational and unitary subject, psychoanalytic theory has been helpful in attempting to explain some of the more seemingly irrational and contradictory aspects of our personalities, especially sexual desire. In labeling her desire as feminine and in valuing romantic love, Goldman was at odds with her more rational or political self that would choose to remake these aspects of conventional femininity. In Goldman's life we witness a philosophical and political commitment to a complete break with traditional norms of femininity combined with what appears as personal sadness over the failure to achieve and maintain what might be considered conventional kinds of feminine–gendered bonds (i.e., within a monogamous love affair or with a child). Here, a psychoanalytic explanation of desire as yearning for unattainable fulfillment—as in the Lacanian analysis—might offer a way of understanding Goldman's lament for an unattainable intimacy she called feminine.

Yet Goldman herself questions the way the feminine has been shaped by social, historical, and economic constraints and never accepted the idea of the feminine as an unshaped or unchanging essence. Goldman never even specified what women might do with a newfound freedom or with the possibility of expressing an authentic feminine desire. She found it more important for her audiences to understand that gender inequity structures the world to severely limit women's freedom than to specify what women might do or what women might want once they have the opportunities. Goldman consistently emphasized the importance of the theatrical and the performative in appealing to audiences, sparking their untapped radicalism and jolting their political consciousness. In her work to move people to action, Goldman (1969b) stressed the importance of the utopian dimension of her thought. She was certain that to rouse social discontent with current conditions, an appeal must be launched to "both mind and heart" (p. 17). Goldman counted herself among the "real revolutionist[s], the dreamer[s], the creative artist[s], the iconoclast[s] in whatever line" (Goldman 1987, 51–52). Her searing critique of current political–economic–social conditions promised a new vision, what she called a "beautiful ideal" of a new society where the human spirit would be free of oppression and restored to dignity and worth. Her vision was that of a feminist anarchist future where all would be free in love and work to develop themselves as fully human and creative beings.

Given this focus on the performative, Goldman would agree with feminist theorists such as Stevi Jackson (2001, 260), who reminds us "our subjectivities, including that aspect of them we call emotions, are shaped by the social and cultural milieu we inhabit, through processes which involve our active engagement with sets of meaning available in our culture." Lauren Berlant (2000, 2), too, emphasizes the material, cultural, and historical context which structures how our most intimate relationships get played out. She notes the mix of fantasy and materiality in stressing the importance of understanding "how to articulate the ways the utopian, optimism-sustaining versions of intimacy meet the normative practices, fantasies, institutions, and ideologies that organize people's worlds." Goldman's life and theory serves as a case study of the ways her desire for a new kind of intimacy and longing for the beautiful dream of her anarchist vision were to butt up against the harsh reality of the lack of community, material, and psychological support needed for her vision to transpire. At the same time that Goldman delivered an anarchist dream of woman's desire to be free from oppressive social conditions and expectations, she could only hint at how this revolution might create a space for new forms of intimacy and specifically how a newly liberated feminine desire might be articulated within these changes.

Central to this though, as I argue throughout this chapter, was Goldman's commitment to the free expression of sexuality. She was as disillusioned with normative conceptions of desire and femininity as she was with the elusive quest for equality. Though Goldman portrayed her own sexuality as heterosexual and longing for commitment and constancy, her ideal makes space for people to express themselves sexually in whatever way they might desire. Once freed from the grip of normative heterosexuality with its accompanying claims about the conventional family, traditional motherhood, the duties of men and women, and so on, Goldman was convinced that people would invent new and freer ways of expressing themselves in their most intimate relations. Goldman flirted with the idea of having a lesbian love affair—and she may have even done so—with anarchist colleague Almeda Sperry, who clearly adored her (Katz 1992, 523–29).

Reframing the struggle for women's, and indeed human, emancipation in terms that speak to our needs for freedom, Goldman was able to put forward the absolute necessity of freeing women on their own terms without having to sacrifice love or varieties of sexual expression and without reference to male-defined and state-centered notions of equality as the measure by which to judge progress.

Familiarity with Goldman's experience, however, reminds us of the constraints patriarchy imposes on the lives of even the freest-thinking women. Having witnessed the failure to achieve her political ideal in the United States, and completely disillusioned by the revolution in the Soviet Union, nearing the end of her life Goldman was particularly bereft of ideals on which to pin her hopes. In a letter to Berkman written in early 1929, Goldman (1975, 145) related the difficulty of writing her autobiography, having to relive and remember her passions in light of their demise:

> It is not only the writing, it is living through what now lies in ashes and being made aware that I have nothing left in the way of personal relations from all who have been in my life and have torn my heart....I should have known that it would be torture to revive the past. I am now paying for it.

Must the inspirational be accompanied by the terrifying, as Goldman witnessed in Wollstonecraft's life and was fulfilled almost as prophecy in Goldman's? Surely the fact that these two women were able to talk so frankly in letters about dilemmas they experienced as women trying to recreate models of love and sexuality speaks to the necessity of studying the personal alongside the philosophical–political. Goldman (1981, 121) remarked, "Had Mary Wollstonecraft not written a line, her life would have furnished food for thought…but she has given us both, she therefore stands among the world's greatest, a life so deep, so rich, so exquisitely beautiful in her complete humanity."

From studying Goldman's life as it intersects with her philosophy of love, freedom, and sexual expression, we are reminded of the contradictions of feminine desire under conditions of patriarchy as well as the necessity of changing consciousness to embrace new forms of intimacy in our most personal relationships. One important contribution Goldman made is her theorization of feminine desire as distinct from male models of femininity. Important, too, is the fact that Goldman's theory of individual freedom and the centrality of sexual expression and desire for this freedom does not exist as an abstract concept untethered by social–political change. Her utopian vision of a feminist future, though unrealized in her own historical moment, might inspire us to move forward. Engaging in the work of feminist genealogy is to learn from the experience, disappointments, and theoretical inspiration of women who have come before us. This represents one step toward breaking the cycle of endless repetition of the same battles. Goldman's life represents the difficulty, as well as the necessity, of believing in a feminist future that can inspire new visions of freedom.

6. Maternal Genealogies and Feminist Consciousness

Simone de Beauvoir on Mothers,
Daughters, and Political Coalitions

The relationships of women to their mothers and to other women—thus toward themselves—are subject to total narcissistic "black-out": these relationships are completely devalued. Indeed, I have never come across a woman who does not suffer from the problem of not being able to resolve in harmony, in the present system, her relationship with her mother and with other women.

Luce Irigaray (1990, 95)

Discussing her decision to forego motherhood, Simone de Beauvoir noted that "mother–daughter relationships are generally catastrophic" (Schwarzer 1984, 91). In the epigraph for this chapter, Luce Irigaray (1990) speaks precisely to this observation. Irigaray lamented the devaluation of vertical relationships between women—mothers and daughters—arguing that women must reclaim their female genealogies to act ethically and politically in establishing horizontal relationships of sisterhood.[1]

I want to begin with and extend this insight by discussing ways feminists have received Beauvoir as a mother of feminism. I do not intend to undertake an exhaustive inventory of Beauvoir's reception among feminists. Instead, I read specific instances in Beauvoir's auto-biography and autobiographical novels alongside her writings about motherhood and *A Very Easy Death*, the moving account of her own mother's deterioration and death, to explore Beauvoir's descriptions of the contradictions and ambivalence women experience in performing their femininity. I focus particularly on difficulties women, including Beauvoir, encounter in breaking free from conventional confines of femininity to claim authentic freedom. I am especially interested in asking how daughters, including feminist daughters of Beauvoir, expe-rience their mothers' struggles within social and political conditions of patriarchy. I argue that what Irigaray (1990) called "black-out" hin-ders feminist consciousness. Routine devaluation of female genealogy blinds us to the historical roots and complexities that influence our relationships to our mothers, to other women, to ourselves, and even to canonical women thinkers such as Beauvoir.

Beauvoir as Feminist Mother

Varieties of mother–daughter tensions arise in an especially acute way in regard to Beauvoir as a feminist mother. Yolanda Patterson (1986, 90) reminds us that Beauvoir "laughingly" dismissed the idea that many feminists looked to her as a mother figure, noting "people don't tend to listen to what their mothers are telling them." Patterson also acknowl-edged, however, that after Beauvoir's death several articles proclaimed her "the mother of the women's movement, the mother of all liberated women, whether or not they knew her name or her work" (ibid.).

When feminists claim Beauvoir as a feminist mother, we are confronted with a complex legacy detailed not only in philosophical work but also in novels and autobiography. Through her letters, autobiography, and autobiographical fiction, Beauvoir deliberately opened up her life for others to scrutinize. In this work, contemporary feminists can witness how Beauvoir experienced and interpreted the complexities of her roles as woman, philosopher, and feminist.[2] The self-exploration that Beauvoir exhibited throughout her life is especially interesting when considered in the midst of what the *Women's Review of Books* (1966) called the "memoir boom."[3] Nancy K. Miller notes the prolificacy of memoir as a genre for women writers and academic critics as a "renewed urgency to add the story of our lives to the public record" (Miller 1997, 982). Looking to Beauvoir's record of her life as a twentieth-century feminist philosopher has served as both inspiration and warning to feminists, especially in the years since her death.

Contemporary feminism's relationship to the legacy of Beauvoir's philosophy, life, and choices reflects deep divisions in regard to the reigning feminist debates on the significance of women's bodies, "feminine" sensibility, and the project of deciding whether "women" are the subject of feminism. Beauvoir's questions and choices remain at the heart of these controversial and pressing issues. Under what conditions can women give voice to their desires individually as well as collectively? Can we even speak of women?[4] Is it possible to identify and act on a feminine desire independent of the male construction of femininity?[5] Probing themes of conventional femininity as experienced by both Beauvoir and the women she created in her fiction marks a return to our symbolic mother to reexamine continuing questions of freedom and choice in feminist politics.

Beauvoir's own experience of being a woman can be studied in her autobiographical fiction as well as in correspondence to friends and lovers. In fiction, she created a number of women who are vulnerable, dependent, and conventionally feminine, as well as women who strive to be independent but are continually in a state of turmoil brought on by the quest for this goal. The intense difficulty a woman experiences in becoming a desiring subject, for example, is vividly illustrated in Beauvoir's (1982) novel *She Came to Stay.* Here we meet Françoise, the central character, struggling to define herself and negotiate her desires in relationship to three central persons in her life: Pierre, Xavière, and Gerbert. The situation in the novel—that of a sexual triangle—was documented by Beauvoir and also by her biographer, Dierdre Bair, as based on the real-life sexual triangle among Beauvoir (Françoise), Sartre (Pierre), and Olga Kosakiewitch (Xavière). Kosakiewitch, a fifteen-year-old student of Beauvoir's in 1933 when Beauvoir was twenty-five, eventually married Jacques-Laurent Bost—portrayed in the novel as Gerbert—an important student of Sartre's and good friend to both Sartre and Beauvoir. Françoise's seduction of Gerbert, enacting in literature Beauvoir's seduction of Bost, is an excellent example of a woman's difficulty in giving voice to her own desire even once she has recognized it.

Françoise, an independent and exceptional woman in every way, is quite able to recognize her desire, but given the constraints of how men and women are to behave in a patriarchal society, can she act on it? Her once "vague yearning" for Gerbert turns into a "choking desire" (Beauvoir 1982, 362). Françoise soon realizes that she would have to make the first move. "Owing to his youth and the respect he had always shown Pierre and herself, she could hardly expect him to take the initiative" (p. 366). "She had always disregarded her dreams and her desires, but this self-effacing wisdom now revolted her....Why did she not make up her mind to will what she hoped for?" (p. 364). Françoise begins a conversation about the virtues of love and friendship. Gerbert claims that with a woman he cannot be himself: "You can't go walking, you can't get drunk, or anything...I prefer it when I can be just what I am with people" (p. 366). Françoise assures Gerbert that he can be just who he is with her. "Oh you! You're like a man!" Gerbert replies. Of course Françoise is an exceptional woman, but that hardly makes her just like a man.[6]

Exploring her options on how to approach Gerbert, Françoise thinks about a friend's experience with men. She, "a woman who takes" (Beauvoir 1982, 368), had affairs with many men, but to no satisfaction. Françoise "loathed the thought" (ibid.) of acting in such an aggressive manner; likewise "she could not bear that he should give in to her out of kindness" (ibid.). The stakes in the dilemma are high. Beauvoir (1989, 686) wrote in *The Second Sex*, "It continues to be more difficult for a woman than for a man to establish the relations with the other sex that she desires. Her erotic and affectional life encounters numerous difficulties. In this matter the unemancipated woman is in no way privileged: sexually and affectionally most wives and courtesans are deeply frustrated. If the difficulties are more evident in the case of the independent woman, it is because she has chosen battle rather than resignation."

Even more difficulties arise when the woman desires another woman in a male-dominated society. How is it possible that a woman could be a desiring subject when "the common opinion" is that "it is the man who conquers, who *has* the woman...it is not admitted that

she, like a man, can have desires of her own: she is the prey of desire"
(Beauvoir 1989, 690). Though neither Beauvoir's autobiography nor
She Came to Stay acknowledges her sexual relationship with Olga
Kosakiewitch, Beauvoir's 1939 journal records relationships with three
women, all émigrées from Eastern Europe: Kosakiewitch, Louise
Védrine, and Natalie Sorokine (Simons 1999, 130). Despite the fact
that Beauvoir (1989) was not open about these aspects of her own
sexuality, she took a very progressive attitude in *The Second Sex*. Of
lesbianism, she wrote, "It is an attitude chosen in a certain situation—
that is, at once motivated and freely adopted. No one of the factors
that mark the subject in connection with this choice—physiological
conditions, psychological history, social circumstances—is the deter-
mining element, though they all contribute to its explanation. It is one
way, among others, in which woman solves the problems posed by her
condition in general, by her erotic situation in particular" (p. 424).

Lesbianism is considered an authentic choice, as "one attempt
among others to reconcile her [woman's] autonomy with the passivity
of her flesh" (Beauvoir 1989, 407). "The great mistake of the psycho-
analysts is, through moralistic conformity, to regard it as never other
than an inauthentic attitude" (p. 406). Scholars studying Beauvoir's
relationship with women find that they disrupt the boundaries of
Beauvoir's heterosexual gender identity (see Simons 1992). Though
She Came to Stay has often been read in terms of the difficulty the
heterosexual couple encounters with the addition of a third party
(see Barnes 1998), when we look beyond the heterosexual matrix, the
novel's perspective changes. We have already noted that Françoise has
tremendous difficulty voicing her desire for Gerbert. She has even
more trouble recognizing and acting on her desire for Xavière. Out on

the town together, arm in arm "for [Xavière] did not dislike having people take them for a couple when they entered a place" (Beauvoir 1982, 246), Françoise wonders about her feelings for this younger woman: "Dancing had made her head spin a little. She felt Xavière's beautiful warm breasts against her, she inhaled her sweet breath. Was this desire? But what did she desire? Her lips against hers? Her body surrendered in her arms? She could think of nothing. It was only a confused need to keep forever this lover's face turned toward hers, and to be able to say with passion: 'She is mine'" (ibid.).

Even more pained than in her encounter with Gerbert, Françoise is at a complete loss with Xavière. She desires Xavière, yet she is unable to imagine reciprocity. "How could she love me?" thinks Françoise with pain. Frozen, unable to act, she worries over the consequences of her inability to be a fully desiring subject (Beauvoir 1982, 248). "Had she [Xavière] hoped that Françoise would compel and force her love on her?" (ibid.). "What exactly did she want? Françoise had to guess; she had to guess everything: what Pierre felt, what was good, what was evil, and what she herself really and truly wanted. Françoise emptied her glass. She saw nothing clearly anymore, nothing at all. Shapeless wreckage lay all about her; within her a great emptiness and darkness throughout" (p. 249).

The evening ends with Françoise feeling dismayed, confused, and disappointed. In writing of feminine sexuality, Beauvoir (1989) described the erotic situation of the woman to be characterized by a fundamental ambiguity. She held that woman's eroticism is much more "complex" than the male's, reflecting "the complexity of the feminine situation." (p. 372). As Eva Gothlin (1999) clarified, Beauvoir spoke of feminine desire as an appeal or a calling out to the other, a desire to be both subject and object, and to be within a relationship of mutual reciprocity and intersubjectivity (see also Lundren-Gothlin 1996). This definition of feminine desire, which marks a connection between an ethical position and the situation of women, is for Beauvoir a positive description. It is one that characterizes the ambiguity of the human condition and our relationship to freedom in that we are at one and the same time separate as well as interdependent beings. As many feminist theorists have noted, Beauvoir understood freedom to be experienced with others, rather than alone, and as both socially situated and conditioned, as opposed to absolute (see Kruks 1995). The fundamental reality of women's situation is such that she finds herself within structures of oppression; her existence is shaped "not only by her own project but by the practices, institutions, and values of the world into which she is born" (Kruks 1995, 90).

Given such a descriptive and compelling novel showing the difficulty for an emancipated woman to recognize and act on her desire, we might wonder at the difficulty of achieving feminist consciousness in our most intimate relationships. Indeed, posthumous revelations about our feminist mother reveal that not even she could play the part of independent woman all the time, nor did she necessarily want to. After Beauvoir's death in 1986, feminists began to react to significant new information regarding the gaps between Beauvoir's presentation of herself and the self she revealed in private letters and diaries. Though Beauvoir was certainly a model of the independent woman—as a scholar, a feminist, a political activist, and a woman who created new relationships outside of marriage—her struggle to maintain this identity and lifestyle was opened for scrutiny with the publication of private diaries and letters. Her essential relationship with Sartre was the object of study and comment, as were other contingent affairs with both men and women (see Hawthorne 2000).

One of these contingent affairs lasted for five years. In 1947, during her travels to the United States while she was writing *The Second Sex*, Beauvoir met the American writer Nelson Algren, with whom she experienced a passionate love. When Beauvoir's (1998) private letters to Algren were published, feminists were offered a new—and for some, shocking—perspective on Beauvoir's private life as a woman and the complex development of her feminism. Many readers found it troubling that Beauvoir, our icon—a role Beauvoir rejected—seemed sometimes unable to act on her own desires. Some of the passages from these letters indicate that she might have subordinated herself to her demanding lover:

> I have to admit this dependence, and I do so willingly since I love you . . .I should throw everything else away to spend a longer time with you. I could have a room of my own so you could work quietly and be alone when you would wish. And I should be so nice: I'll wash the dishes and mop the floor, and go to buy eggs and rum-cake by myself; I shall not touch your hair or cheek or shoulder without being allowed to do so; I shall try not to be sad when you'll be ill-tempered because of the morning mail or for any other reason; I shall not interfere with your freedom. (p. 71)

Hanging out by the lake in Michigan or in Algren's grungy Chicago apartment "washing the dishes," "mopping the floor," refraining from touching her "husband's" "hair or cheek or shoulder without being allowed to do so" represents a most dramatic contrast with Beauvoir's busy Parisian life as writer, philosopher, editor, and longtime companion of one of the most famous philosophers of the twentieth century. Could Beauvoir have been engaging in her own fantasies of ease, of immanence, and of choosing the easy slopes? Or was she simply being ironic, knowing all the while that she would never think of engaging in such a domestic routine? Maybe the willful performance of the fantasy of immanence helps to remind us of the importance of choosing lives of action and of transcendence. Or, can assuming immanence rather than having it imposed in perpetuity embrace the ambiguity of sexuality and of intimacy?

In light of the flurry of responses to these letters that expressed worry over Beauvoir's choice to conduct her affair with a "macho know-nothing at the very time she was writing *The Second Sex*" (Robinson 1999, 4), we might recall that Beauvoir's own claims about a woman's sexuality and freedom were complex. Even in the letter just mentioned, she demands a room of her own so that Algren can work quietly. It is important to think through Beauvoir's descriptions of the ambiguity of the feminine condition within the context of the way Beauvoir described the dilemmas framing an emancipated woman's life. She had to negotiate the competing demands of love and independence. In the section on "The Independent Woman" in *The Second Sex*, Beauvoir (1989) wrote that man is not divided. The emancipated woman, however, "refuses to confine herself to her role as female, because she will not accept mutilation; but it would also be a mutilation to repudiate her sex" (p. 682). "To renounce her femininity is to renounce a part of her humanity," but what can a woman do when to realize her femininity a woman must make herself "object and prey" (ibid.)?

Beauvoir (1989, 371) convincingly argued that sexuality "is profoundly different—biologically, socially, and psychologically—for man and woman."[7] The woman embodies the ambiguity of the human situation more clearly than does the man, for the woman has difficulty in assuming the role of subject and object.

> The erotic experience is one that most poignantly discloses to human beings the ambiguity of their condition; in it they are aware of themselves as flesh and as spirit, as the other and as subject. This conflict has a more dramatic shape for woman because at first she feels herself to be object and does not at once realize a sure independence in sex enjoyment; she must regain her dignity as transcendent and free subject while assuming her carnal condition—an enterprise fraught with difficulty and danger, and one that often fails. (p. 402)

Sexual relations constitute an especially interesting test for women's subjectivity in that woman, though used to being a sexual object, must become a desiring subject to enjoy the carnal act. In this sense, woman is especially "divided against herself" (p. 377). Indeed, how can women become sexual subjects when it is considered obscene to speak of woman's desire?[8] At the same time, the ambiguity of the erotic situation reveals that women must sometimes willingly make themselves objects to enjoy the sex act. As Beauvoir clarified, "To *make* oneself an object, to *make* oneself passive, is a very different thing from *being* a passive object" (p. 379). Feminine desire, as Gothlin (1999, 89) characterized it, is for Beauvoir a situation in which "you are both subject and object, with the limits separating you and me as both there and erased."

Yet the question remains: Are women offered, and can they seize, the opportunities to express desire and affirm their subjectivity under patriarchy? Is it even possible to speak of women as desiring subjects—and as desiring to make themselves passive rather than be objects—when women have only been spoken of as objects of male desire? And most importantly, could exploring these contradictions of feminine desire—those of our mothers and our feminist mothers—help us to articulate a feminist consciousness? I argue that feminist consciousness might arise from comprehending and situating women's concrete similarities in regard to the difficulties of giving voice to our desires. This begins with a reclaiming of feminist genealogy.

Simone and Françoise

Luce Irigaray (1993c, 9) asked and answered a fundamental question about Beauvoir: "So what did Simone de Beauvoir do? She gave an account of her own life while backing it up scientifically. She never stopped recounting it, bravely, at every stage. In so doing she helped many women—and men?—to be more free sexually, especially by offering them a sociocultural role model, acceptable at that time, of a woman's life, a teacher's life, a writer's life, and the life of a couple. I think she also helped them to situate themselves more objectively in relation to different moments in life."

Most of all, Beauvoir demonstrated that for the independent woman in patriarchal society, movement toward a life of transcendence and freedom is experienced in tension with the temptation to simply accept and perpetuate the conventional life that society has chosen as appropriate for women.[9] Daughters experience these contradictions in looking to the lives of their mothers, just as feminists experience contradictory emotions in reading the life of Beauvoir. Uma Narayan (1997, 10) articulated that mothers, mother-cultures, and feminist mothers inspire "complicated emotional responses from their feminist daughters—love and fear, the desire to repudiate and the desire to understand and be understood, a sense of deep connection and a desperate desire for distance." Contradictory pulls between feminist consciousness and feminine destiny are manifested in our response. Beauvoir (1989, 679–715) noted the dilemma for the "independent woman" as that between "human" freedom and her "feminine" destiny. How can we articulate a feminist response?

Beauvoir turned to her mother's story, where we meet Beauvoir's mother, Françoise, to probe more deeply into her own. Narayan (1997) wrote of the difficulty of weaving a mother's story into one's own, telling it faithfully while also creating the space to claim one's own history and subjectivity.[10] "Telling the story of a person whose life is intertwined with one's own, in terms different from her own, is often a morally delicate project, requiring accommodation and tact and an ability to leave room for her account even as one claims room for one's own" (p. 9). How can one write the story of the mother, subject as we are to intergenerational rage and resentment? Drucilla Cornell (2002, xix, 24) argued that feminist attempts at "multicultural, intracultural, and transnational dialogues between women" would be greatly enhanced in facing up to this "intergenerational haunting between women." The haunting, manifested in a "grim wasteland of broken spirits, victims of their own internalized oppression" (p. xx), must be explored as a common thread in women's lives. This exploration could turn broken dreams into dignity and hope for our daughters that they may be propelled to realize greater freedom for themselves.

Within a searing critique of conventional ideals of motherhood, Beauvoir was able to reclaim her mother's dignity in recounting her story as work on female genealogy. She symbolized her relationship with her mother in a way that allowed her mother the space to be both a mother and a woman; this marks Beauvoir's essay as engaged in the feminist work of reimagining our relationships with our mothers. I argue that Beauvoir's work allows us to rethink motherhood in vital and feminist ways. It frees women from competing for the unique place occupied by the mother; it frees women to differentiate themselves from their mothers; and it frees women from forever being reduced to the maternal function (see Whitford 1991, 75–97).

To situate Beauvoir in relationship to maternal genealogies may appear, at first glance, counterintuitive. Indeed, feminist scholars have documented and debated the ambivalence Beauvoir demonstrated in regard to femininity and the female body.[11] Criticism has focused on her negative description of female biological functions such as menstruation, lactation, pregnancy, and maternity. Many cite Beauvoir as male identified and as abhorring the female body. Others document that Beauvoir interrogated biological descriptions of sexuality, offering an alternative description of female biology as constituted within situation, and a historical, sociological, political, and economic context (Arp 1995; Ward 1995).

In the view I offer here of Beauvoir's (1989, 34) description of maternity and the mother–daughter bond in particular, Beauvoir is understood to be discussing the body not as a thing but as a situation. Beauvoir made clear that the body is always lived in by the subject; the meaning biological "facts" take on is "dependent on a whole context" (ibid.). As examples, Beauvoir undermined the naturalness or inevitability of heterosexuality and reproduction. She insisted, even, that no maternal instinct exists. "The word hardly applies, in any case, to the human species. The mother's attitude depends on her total situation and her reaction to it [and] this is highly variable (p. 511).

Though Beauvoir (1965) made the choice to not become a mother, she wrote of the maternal bond from her perspective as a daughter.

When she discovered that she had to confront her mother's deterioration and death from cancer, her relationship to the female body was
tested in the most personal of contexts. *A Very Easy Death* negotiates
Beauvoir's fear of her mother, of her mother's body, of becoming too
like her mother, of the compulsion toward motherhood and the social
and political roles that govern its expression. Coming into close contact with her mother's body in the hospital horrifies her: "The sight of
my mother's nakedness had jarred me. No body existed less for me:
none existed more. As a child I had loved it dearly; as an adolescent
it had filled me with an uneasy repulsion: all this was perfectly in the
ordinary course of things and it seemed reasonable to me that her body
should retain its dual nature, that it should be both repugnant and
holy—a taboo. But for all that, I was astonished at the violence of my
distress" (pp. 19–20).

Unsurprisingly, Françoise de Beauvoir made frequent appearances
in her daughter's dreams: "She blended with Sartre, and we were
happy together. And then the dream would turn into a nightmare:
Why was I living with her once more? How had I come to be in her
power again? So our former relationship lived on in me in its double
aspect—a subjection that I loved and hated. It revived with all its
strength when Maman's accident, her illness, and her death shattered
the routine that then governed our contacts (Beauvoir 1965, 103).

Beauvoir's experience of her own femininity as well as her political
choices can be said to be framed by her rejection of the life trajectory
of her conventional mother. Beauvoir found maternal love comforting
and whole but also oppressive, suffocating, a threat to her own—the
daughter's—sense of self. Beauvoir feared that a life spent redefining the

meaning of being a woman, philosophically and personally, could be jeopardized by the paralysis and fear she felt in her mother's presence.

Simultaneously, though, Beauvoir was inspired by her mother's life; the very constraints contained within it shaped her to desire something different. In autobiographical writings Beauvoir recounted that her mother was always a model, usually one she did not wish to emulate. Elaine Marks (1973, 101) noted that one might "sense that [Beauvoir's] revolt against the despicable bourgeoisie is, in part, an outgrowth of her revolt against Françoise de Beauvoir." Witnessing her mother's work in the home and seeing her personality strangled taught the dutiful daughter to desire another kind of life. "One afternoon I was helping Mama to wash up; she was washing the plates, and I was drying; through the window I could see the wall of the barracks, and other kitchens in which women were scrubbing out saucepans or peeling vegetables. Every day lunch and dinner; every day washing-up; all those hours, those endlessly recurring hours, all leading nowhere: could I live like that?" (Beauvoir 1986, 104)

The hardships of her mother's life, the constant denial of her desire, and the effects that denial had on herself and her sister made Beauvoir firm in the belief that she would reject that life trajectory. In her *Memoirs of a Dutiful Daughter*, it is clear that Beauvoir (1986, 140–41) saw motherhood as a kind of trap with the potential to suck her back into the bourgeois existence she so feared and loathed:

> I had long ago decided to devote my life to intellectual labours. Zaza
> shocked me when she declared, in a provocative tone of voice: "Bringing
> nine children into the world as Mama has done is just as good as writing
> books." I couldn't see any common denominator between these two modes
> of existence. To have children, who in their turn would have more children,
> was simply to go on playing the same old tune *ad infinitum*; the scholar, the

artist, the writer, and the thinker created other worlds, all sweetness and
light, in which everything had purpose.

The very fact that her mother's life consisted of a daily denial of what
Beauvoir (1965, 36) called "awkward truths" was enough to convince
her that "bourgeois marriage is an unnatural institution." Years of
betrayal by her husband, compounded by having to "give up many
of the things she had dreamt of" (p. 34) took its toll on Françoise de
Beauvoir's spontaneity. When the mother is taught to deny her own
desire, the maternal can ultimately be nothing other than a space of
confinement and repression. Beauvoir remembered an expression her
mother would often use, one that the family found vexing: She began
her sentences, "I certainly have the right" (p. 39). Beauvoir surmised
that this phrase revealed her mother's "want of self-assurance" and that
"her desires did not carry their own justification with them" (ibid.). As
Beauvoir put it, her mother "lived against herself": "She had appetites
in plenty: she spent all her strength in repressing them and she under-
went this denial in anger. In her childhood her body, her heart, and
her mind had been squeezed into an armour of principles and prohi-
bitions. She had been taught to pull the laces hard and tight herself.
A full-blooded, spirited woman lived on inside her, but a stranger to
herself, deformed and mutilated" (pp. 42–43).

Beauvoir wondered how things would have been different with her
mother had she lived her life as a free and desiring subject. Beauvoir
(1965, 50) recalled her mother's spontaneous smile, exhibited far too
infrequently, that ironically returned at the moment of sure death:
"Both of us, my sister and I, had the same thought: it was that same
smile that had dazzled us when we were little children, the radiant

smile of a young woman. Where had it been between then and now?" The young Simone linked that smile with her parents' love, thinking it was "associated in some mysterious way with that bedroom she had just left" (p. 34). But steadily, Beauvoir's mother had eased herself into a "successful marriage, two daughters who loved her dearly, some degree of affluence," hardly regretting that her husband's "wishes always came before hers," becoming quite capable of "selfless devotion" (pp. 34–35). Despite being "cut off from the pleasures of the body, deprived of the satisfactions of vanity, tied down to wearisome tasks that bored and humiliated her" (p. 37), Françoise de Beauvoir kept up a "forced optimism" (p. 38). Eventually, the Beauvoir family's declining fortune forced Simone's mother to look after the house without a servant. Beauvoir reported that her mother loathed the housework: "It is a pity that out-of-date ideas should have prevented her from adopting the solution she came round to twenty years later—that of working away from the home" (p. 35). Wishing her mother could have experienced this slight degree of freedom, Beauvoir lamented that "she would have escaped a degree of dependence that tradition made her think natural but that did not in the least agree with her nature" (p. 36).

This insight—that freedom is constituted by situation—is aptly demonstrated in the analysis (1965) Beauvoir applied to her own mother's life. Had the situation for women in WWI France been more open, had Simone's mother been forced to go to work, had she come around herself to the solution of working away from the home earlier, she might have been "better equipped to bear the frustration that she had to put up with" (p. 36). In fact, Françoise might have been a totally different kind of mother had her situation been different.

Can Beauvoir Teach Us about Political Coalition?

Beauvoir neglected to speak of a political strategy that would spur women toward a movement of emancipation, concentrating instead on individual difficulties women experience in recognizing themselves as complete and whole subjects able to desire love, freedom, even sexual satisfaction. Indeed, Michèle Le Doeuff (2000, 43) noted, "The American Women's Liberation Movement, the French MLF of the 1970s and their equivalents in the other developed countries have not necessarily regarded *The Second Sex* [or Beauvoir's other works] as their *What Is To Be Done?*...nor would [Beauvoir] have liked it if they had." If this is the conclusion, then what did Beauvoir have to say to feminists today? What can feminists learn from Beauvoir?

In marking out our own desires to transcend woman's body as inessential object and in articulating woman's desire to constitute herself as a desiring subject, Beauvoir simultaneously showed us how to be a woman subject among other women. Offering us her life as a model and her work as a collection of philosophy, fiction, and autobiography, and breathing life into the experiences of countless other women, Beauvoir showed us how to perceive ourselves as women in the company of the experiences of other women. Though gender "is not always constituted coherently or consistently in different historical contexts," and "gender intersects with racial, class, ethnic, sexual, and regional identities" (Butler 1990, 3), the study of Beauvoir's life and work presents the possibility of understanding the conditions that produce diversity as well as those that establish the possibility of a unity of women. Le Doeuff (2000) has called this a kind of "minimum consensus":

One can know oneself as a woman by being among women and through concern about what happens to other or to all women. Thus we saw lesbians joining in the struggle for contraception and abortion on demand, women who had the means to "get by" anyway calling for their legalization and reimbursement by social security, women without children setting up organizations for building crèches, single women showing their concern for the daily problems of housewives, and Western women being appalled by clitoridectomy or the forced wearing of the chador. This is what replaced nail varnish and the acknowledgement of the lord and master in women's consciousness of self: a sense of being women because they wanted more freedom, a better life, and dignity for all women. (pp. 45–46)

When Beauvoir framed women's desires in terms of the reaching out toward freedom and the obstacles encountered in that reaching—as well as how situation affects the possibility of reaching out—she returned us to a paradigm of seeking freedom on women's own terms rather than seeking equality on male terms. Reading *The Second Sex*, Beauvoir's novels, and her letters, we are invited into the company of scores of women, along with Beauvoir herself, engaged in seeking freedom while butting up against conventions of femininity. Describing ourselves as women under these circumstances does not demand that we inscribe certain characteristics to feminine desire, nor does it indicate anything essential about being a woman. Instead, it calls us to see ourselves as part of a community of beings who are blocked on the path to freedom. Moreover, it asks us to come together as a community seeking freedom without offering up a blueprint of how that might be accomplished or under whose name one might gather.

We might think of Beauvoir's discomfort with her mother's choices—as well as our own uneasy relationship to Beauvoir's choices—in light of the way she articulates the difficulty of choosing freedom and the attraction of the easy slopes. For Beauvoir, her mother's body represents immanence, decay, and the impossibility of transcendence, as well as the domain of choices her mother made or failed to make. The violence of Beauvoir's distress, however, does not manifest itself in repulsion for her mother, the Other within herself. Rather than seek to expel the Other, especially at this dangerous moment of recognition, Beauvoir (1965) felt compassion. She wrote, "I talked to Sartre about my mother's mouth as I had seen it that morning and about everything I had interpreted in it—greediness refused, an almost servile humility, hope, distress, loneliness—the loneliness of her death and her life—that did not want to admit its existence. And he told me that my own mouth was not obeying me any more: I had put Maman's mouth on my own face and in spite of myself, I copied its movements. Her whole person, her whole being, was concentrated there, and compassion wrung my heart" (p. 31).

Here Beauvoir recognized that she has her mother's mouth "in spite of" herself; it even copies the movements of its progenitor. She struggled with her relationship to her mother, thinking through her mother's limited choices as well as the constraints of the body, in much the same way feminists have had to deal with Beauvoir's legacy. Certain discomforts are aroused when we are suddenly faced with the fact that Beauvoir the feminist also struggled with understanding her mother's life and resisting conventional models of femininity. In Beauvoir's life, we witness the uncomfortable reality that ontological freedom never exists independently of social and political freedom.

In *The Second Sex*, Beauvoir (1989, xxv) emphasized that freedom cannot be gained through personal choice but only through a process of complex social transformation. In her introduction, she speculated on why women do not say "we" in regard to ourselves and our common interests: "Women lack concrete means for organizing themselves into a unit that can stand face to face with the correlative unit. They have no past, no history, no religion of their own; and they have no such solidarity of work and interest as that of the proletariat....They live dispersed among the males, attached through residence, housework, economic condition, and social standing to certain men—fathers or husbands—more firmly than they are to other women."

Women are dispersed among various classes and races; they have no past, no history, no religion of their own. These racial and class attachments prevent women from organizing into a unified movement under the singular umbrella of *woman*. Moreover, and possibly most importantly, women's emotional attachments seem to separate them from each other, often attaching them to certain men—their husbands, their brothers, their sons, their fathers. These subjective–psychological aspects of women's emotional bonds reinforce the objective aspects of women's oppression. Choosing freedom, it turns out, is an arduous task, next to impossible for the individual woman. As Kruks (1987, 117) put it, "If woman is to become a free existent (and indeed if male freedom is to be increased), the process of change will have to commence from the radical transformation of the institutional aspects of woman's situation. Marriage, motherhood, her exclusion from economic and public activity, all will have to be extensively transformed."

I suggest here that the transformation might begin with the recognition of common struggles women encounter. Irigaray (1993b) called this acknowledgment "sisterhood," but Audre Lorde (1982, 81) cautioned against believing that an invocation of sisterhood will necessarily foster solidarity:

At home, my mother said, "Remember to be sisters in the presence of strangers." She meant white people, like the woman who tried to make me get up and give her my seat on the Number 4 bus, and who smelled like cleaning fluid. At St. Catherine's, they said, "Be sisters in the presence of strangers," and they meant non-Catholics. In high school, the girls said, "Be sisters in the presence of strangers," and they meant men. My friends said, "Be sisters in the presence of strangers," and they meant the squares. But in high school, my real sisters were strangers; my teachers were racists; and my friends were that color I was never supposed to trust.

Lorde's autobiography forces us to think about location and coalition. In charting the barriers and boundaries she experienced as a woman, a lesbian, and an African American of West Indian descent, she made it clear that sisterhood does not make sense as an abstract or universal concept. As a child, Lorde was taught to see difference as a threat—which it was, within her racist environment—not realizing that one can make coalitions with others unlike oneself. As readers, we witness her struggle to find a new spelling of her name as Zami, the Carriacou name for women who work together as friends and lovers.

Throughout this book, I support the claim that it is essential to investigate literal and metaphorical maternal genealogies to begin to effect the change in consciousness required for women to think of each other as political allies, friends, and lovers. Looking to our mother's lives and the lives and legacies of our feminist mothers acknowledges our vertical bonds, clearing the path toward forging horizontal ones. Beauvoir's struggles in her life—for example with her mother, with sexual attraction, with love, and with conventional definitions of womanhood—might inspire us, publicly and in concert with others, to speculate on the links between feminist consciousness and political transformation. Looking to the lives of other women, our mothers as well as other women whose lives are mostly radically unlike our own, is an instigating factor inspiring feminist consciousness toward transformation. If women could see links between their lives and their mother's lives, themselves and other women, we might avoid the black-out referred to by Irigaray (1990) in the opening epigraph to this chapter. If we understand women's commonality as emanating from struggles to speak our desires and win our freedom rather than as essence or fixed identity, then women, however differently situated as subjects, might act together in common cause to end their shared oppression.

Maybe we expected more from our feminist mother. We should remember Beauvoir's descriptions of the difficulty of offering freedom to one's daughters while continuing to live within male definitions of philosophy, language, and self. Recognizing that we are deeply ensconced in relationships of patriarchy, Irigaray (1993c, 9) urged us to revalue vertical relationships toward the feminist project of positing horizontal ones: "If we are not to be accomplices in the murder of the mother we also need to assert that there is a genealogy of women. Each of us has a female family tree: we have a mother, a maternal grandmother and great-grandmothers, we have daughters."

It may give us pause to realize that Beauvoir (1986) fantasized of being a mother only under conditions in which men were completely absent. "When we played games, I accepted the role of mother only if I were allowed to disregard its nursing aspects....I accepted the discreet collaboration of my sister whom I high-handedly assisted in the bringing up of her own children. But I refused to allow a man to come between me and my maternal responsibilities: our husbands were always abroad" (p. 56). Must husbands be abroad for women to recognize and value their relationships with other women, both vertically—with mothers—and horizontally—with each other? According to the reading of Beauvoir presented here, feminist practice, if it is to be transformative, must posit the relation to the other woman as the privileged interlocutor.

7. Wanting It All

Contemporary Struggles for Freedom and Fulfillment

Throughout this book I argue that feminists must study the complexity of the lives of women, most importantly the feminists who came before us, to recognize the ambivalence each of these women felt about the expectations and demands of being women in their respective historical and cultural contexts. In this chapter, I turn to accounts written by contemporary feminists. As with our feminist predecessors, each story is individual, intimate, and irreplaceably her own. At the same time, however, overarching themes emerge. Many of the struggles articulated are quite similar, and in some cases eerily reminiscent, to those I identified in the work of earlier feminists. In this chapter I rely a bit more heavily on quotations from the authors. Because this work is not as well known as the canonical feminists I work with in previous chapters, I offer longer quotes and place the quotes within their textual context. I hope that by relying more on each woman's own voice I can offer a more complete sense of the dilemmas these feminists confronted within their specific locations. The memoirs that interest me here were written by feminist intellectuals fully conscious of their moment in history, their location within their culture, and their own desire to transcend the meanings of being a woman their society preordained for them. They struggled with remaking their societies, with building communities of women, and with forging feminist consciousness through understanding and redefining their own relationships to their mothers.

The memoirs I explore in the first two sections deal explicitly with political transformations enacted to change material conditions, including those of gender construction. These are accounts of revolutions written by feminist participants that play out within a national and colonial frame. Feminists such as Chandra Mohanty (*Feminism without Borders*, 2004) have called for transnational organizing and a politics of solidarity to craft critical multicultural feminist practice. The memoirs I engage, written within the context of national struggles, make us especially aware of keeping feminist goals, defined through women's engagement in revolutionary struggles, in dialogue with transnational feminist organizing. Giaconda Belli's (2002) memoir documents her participation in the Sandinista Revolution in Nicaragua, whereas Azar Nafisi (2003) recounts the transformations she experienced in her life under the Khomeini regime in Iran. Belli is a celebrated Nicaraguan poet, now living in the United States; Nafisi is an Iranian professor of literature, also now living in the United States and teaching at Johns Hopkins University. Both women infuse their stories with a feminist consciousness of the importance of putting women's needs and the struggles of women's lives at the forefront of any revolutionary praxis. In presenting their experience of how the meanings of being a woman are manipulated for political purposes that serve to confine women to rigid roles, Belli's and Nafisi's memoirs bring Mary Wollstonecraft's and Germaine de Staël's writings on the French Revolution and its betrayal of women into a contemporary focus.

Struggles within Material Conditions

Giaconda Belli grew up as a daughter of the upper class in pre-Sandinista Nicaragua and confided that she tried to live the kind of life the people around her—parents, society, and their class of friends—expected. Belli (2002, 6) wrote, "The wedding was held in February of 1967. I had turned eighteen scarcely two months earlier. I was still a virgin. My satin silk bridal gown was simple, with a tulle overskirt and Venetian lace detailing. I was quite pleased with the way I looked—that is, until my mother arranged the cap and veil upon my head, and guided each of my hands inside a long, kid-skin glove. At that moment, all of a sudden, a sense of ridicule came over me, I felt I was being packaged up like a gift." As Belli explained it, she felt that two different women existed in her: "I have been two women and I have lived two lives. One of these women wanted to do everything by the classic feminine code: get married, have children, be supportive, docile, and nurturing. The other woman yearned for the privileges men enjoyed: independence, self-reliance, a public life, mobility, lovers. I have spent the greater part of my life trying to balance and blend these two identities, to avoid being torn apart by their opposing forces" (pp. ix, x).

The second woman was awakened in Belli by a subversive combination of sexuality and politics. While married to her first husband, Belli met a man she identifies only as "the Poet." He romanced her with poetry and with a new knowledge of the history of her own country. The Poet supplied Belli with readings on General Sandino, the fight against U.S. intervention, and the Somoza dictatorship. This work and the Poet's sure guidance introduced Belli to the beauty and abject misery of Nicaragua while awakening her sensuality: "I was twenty-one. The Poet, twenty-six. That transgression was my personal genesis. It made me question all my obligations, and I began to think seriously about my rights, about what my life was and what it could be. My desire for freedom grew as wide as the universe. What remained of my life as a young, upper-class wife was nothing but appearance. Volcanoes, cataclysms had begun inside" (Belli 2002, 31).

Belli recounts that this transformation stimulated a potent longing for personal and political freedom. As she became increasingly conscious of Nicaragua's harsh political realities and grew committed to the ideals of the Sandinista revolutionaries, Belli also shed conventional bourgeois codes of morality. Throughout the memoir, Belli practiced sexual freedom, fell in love with various men—two of them Sandinista revolutionaries, one of whom loses his life—and married three times. She gave birth to two daughters and a son and adopted a third daughter. We might read this memoir as a manifesto for the successful embrace of both political and personal revolution, were it not for the nagging doubts Belli continually confessed. The life she chose, one of active participation in the Sandinista movement, put her children at risk and forced her to make wrenching choices between family safety and political activism. In this, Belli's narrative is hauntingly reminiscent of Staël's *Ten Years of Exile*. As we recall from chapter 4, Staël was also an upper-class woman who spoke out against political injustice—not out of necessity but because of her ideals. Both Staël and Belli consciously chose to be political and to take the risks that subversive speech and action entail under a dictatorship. As Belli (2002, 76) honestly revealed, "One of the privileges of my social class, I had recently realized, was the unspoken feeling that we were immune. Bad things happened to other people. We, instead, imagined the world as a cozier place and trusted our good fortune. Changing sides meant giving up that internalized sense of security."

However, as both women are fully aware, giving up that sense of security for oneself also entails relinquishing it for those to whom one remains connected. Though, for example, Staël repeatedly asserted her belief in the sacrifices required to stand up to Napoleon Bonaparte, she also confided her doubts about what this political commitment would cost for those close to her. Belli's words are familiar, though more personally explicit than Staël's. Belli worried constantly about her children and how the difficulties of her situation, a situation she had consciously chosen, might affect them.

> Melissa with her pacifier and Maryam with her arms wide open. If only I could take them back into my womb to shelter them. I wanted a womb to hide in with them, the warm safety of the amniotic fluid. At least Nicaragua wasn't like Argentina, or Chile, where the dictatorships tortured and killed children along with their parents. I didn't fear for their lives—what I feared was the idea of them being left all alone. Did I have any right, as a mother, to take such risks? That question gnawed away at me for years, like an accusatory finger, the gesture with which my mother always scolded me. But my fate was already sealed. Inside of me there wasn't the slightest impulse to turn back. A threat like this, in fact, had the opposite effect: it fed the rage I felt for the dictatorship, for a system against which we, the citizens, had no form of defense. Ever since the earthquake the country had been placed under a state of siege. Our constitutional rights were suspended. Nobody protested, mainly because we had already been living like that long before it was officially declared. Then and there, I vowed to myself that I wouldn't allow fear to turn me into a passive observer of all the ills and injustices that surrounded me. It would do me good, I thought, to experience in my own

flesh and blood the kind of vulnerability my fellow countrymen lived with every day. It was essential in any struggle to withstand the obstacles, to persevere. Otherwise we would never be able to realize our dreams. If I gave in to fear, I would end up killing my soul to save my body. I barely slept that night, not even taking my clothes off. I was afraid of knocks at the door. Of the men, and the thought that they could drag me outside, beat me in front of my daughters. (p. 78)

Like Staël, Belli remained intensely committed to her beliefs while admitting self-doubt. This theme dominates the memoir. Belli never congratulated herself on her political commitments and the sacrifices they required without lamenting the way her family was forced to suffer the consequences.

I'd try to explain to my kids what I was doing, telling them about poverty, needy children, and the obligation to be responsible to other people. I think I sounded like some missionary nun as I tried to explain the scope of a commitment that went beyond our individual happiness. For the love of the many, for a future where things could be fair for everyone, I had to temporarily sacrifice being with them.

For them there was no other palpable reality than their mother's absence. "Are you my mommy from the airplane?" Melissa would ask me. Maryam, who unwittingly had turned into my mother's spokesperson, would exacerbate my guilt with her reproachful, pained tone. In her childish handwriting, my poor little girl even wrote me a letter declaring that maybe there were poor children in the world, but at least they had their mothers. (p. 127)

Because the contradictions are so acute and so powerful, Belli's memoir demonstrates how hard it is to play out the roles of woman and revolutionary or woman and political activist simultaneously. Conventional models of femininity leave little room for acting in light of political ideals, but Belli insistently wanted it all: "Revolutionary dreams found fertile ground in my young mind, as did other, more conventional kinds of dreams, although my knights in shining armor were guerrillas and my heroic exploits would be performed between changing diapers and boiling baby bottles" (p. ix). These were her dreams. Belli confessed that in real life these two kinds of existence did not blend as easily, though she occasionally had remarkable success. She was able, for example, to assemble her first "underground Sandinista network" amid "a world of soiled diapers, Melissa's colicky cries, and daily struggles to placate Maryam's newfound jealousy of her baby sister" (p. 62). But even after the Revolution was victorious, the work was unceasing, and the commitment was implacable.

> Sleep deprived and depressed, I dragged myself through militia training sessions, night watches, volunteer work in storm drains, and Sundays picking cotton under the hot sun during the harvest. There were moments when I was happy. I especially enjoyed the camaraderie of volunteer work, being in the back of a truck returning from the fields, singing the tunes I had sung in exile when the idea of triumph seemed distant or far-fetched. But I'd come home to face my daughters' recriminations.
>
> "Mommy, you said that when we won the Revolution we would have more time to be together."
>
> "But there's so much to do," I would say. "Things will get back to normal soon. Just be patient."
>
> But I said it without conviction. I didn't have the faintest idea of when the situation would normalize, or when we would have more time together. (p. 295)

With lovers and husbands, too, models of conventional femininity would clash with her desire to be a different kind of woman. Sometimes Belli admits that this was partially her own fault, her internalized acceptance of being "taught to please...trained to be chameleons for our men, adapting to them" (p. 341). As a result, she felt that she could not be independent in the way she would like. "I didn't know how to be alone. I had exposed myself to bullets, death; I had smuggled weapons, given speeches, received awards, had children—so many things, but a life without men, without love, was alien to me, I felt I had no existence unless a man's voice said my name and a man's love rendered my life worthwhile" (p. 290).

More often, though, it was the men in her life, even men of the Revolution, who failed to understand what a transformation in gender roles meant for their own sense of who they were as men. Here Belli's narrative is reminiscent of issues Emma Goldman faced. The men in Belli's life struggled with accepting her new ways of being a woman while the Revolution struggled to live up to its own ideals of giving women the place they deserved and fought for.

> For the first time ever, I heard someone suggest that perhaps women should be barred from active service. I considered that ludicrous and said so. How could they even think such a thing when women had already proven themselves to be as able fighters as men during the insurrection? Nevertheless, some months later, the top army officials, led by Humberto Ortega, decided that from that point on women would only occupy administrative posts. They justified the decision by saying it was a question of money, that keeping men and women soldiers separate was a giant headache that incurred far too many additional expenses. But the Sandinista police, as it was called then, which was being organized with advisers supplied by General Torrijos, chose not to make that distinction and women enlisted in its ranks in great numbers. The same thing happened in the Ministry of the Interior. I liked seeing those women in their olive green uniforms and impeccably shined military boots. Many of them wore lipstick and even painted their nails bright red. These were all signs of a new era for the women in my country. (p. 262)

Sadly but predictably, the Sandinista Revolution failed to live up to the promises it made to its female participants. As a representative of the Sandinista government, Belli traveled to Algeria where she found that the experience of her feminist comrades there taught them women were easily forgotten once the Revolution was won: "I was interviewed by a number of female journalists who wanted to know if in Nicaragua the men would cast aside the women who had participated in the Revolution, as they had in Algeria. Their lot was better than that of women in other Arab countries, but they still had to fight tooth and nail to avoid constantly being pushed to the sidelines. I told them that their experience, and that of many other women as well, would serve as a warning sign to us, to help us keep from being sent back to the kitchens, to the margins. They could hardly mask their skepticism. We'll see, their expressions seemed to say" (p. 281).

In Libya, Belli was asked by her high-ranking Sandinista lover, Modesto, to sit at a separate table from other members of the Nicaraguan delegation. She angrily recalled, "According to the Koran, women don't have souls, Modesto explained to me, laughing at my fury that they, my *compañeros*, would allow such a thing. "This is another culture, come on, don't be like that," he said, trying to calm me down. But we too were another culture—why not tell that to the Libyans?" (p. 284). And, as the final insult, Belli was questioned by the Sandinista leadership about her lover, Charlie, an American journalist in Nicaragua, a man she eventually married and lives with in the United States. A conversation with her cousin offered the perspective Belli needed.

> Hadn't I noticed that my male *compañeros* were never questioned about the female company they kept? Was I not aware that even those who had jobs far more sensitive than my own slept with foreign women, women journalists, whoever they felt like sleeping with? Perhaps I didn't know that the chief of one of the State Security divisions was married to a gringa? The same went for other men she mentioned, all of them holding important government positions. She was on a roll and kept at it. Are you trying to tell me that after so

many years risking your skin for the Revolution, you're just simply going to sit back and calmly accept their lack of trust? That you will accept without flinching the insulting notion that because you are a woman you can't keep your head when you drop your underwear? A bunch of self-righteous male chauvinists, that's what they are! That's all there is to it! (p. 325)

Butting up against conventional conceptions of femininity was not as surprising for Belli as the realization that she was unconsciously accepting these notions. It takes a push from a *compañera*, her cousin Pía, for Belli to understand that she was being subject to gender regulations and that her male comrades completely escaped such scrutiny: "How could I, who was the feminist militant, have not thought of all these things until Pía brought them up? It was embarrassing. Pía was right. I had reacted in a most traditional way, accepting, without a whimper, prejudices about women that dated from the time when Adam bit the apple. I jumped up and hugged her. I love women, I thought. We had to stick together so that men's ideas about our 'duties,' what we could or couldn't do, wouldn't cloud our thinking. It was good to remember that political power, even when it was considered revolutionary, had been for the most part a man's job, tailored to his needs" (p. 326).

Communities of Women

Like Belli, Nafisi (2003) also learned the hard way the importance of women sticking together. After years of increasing controls and regulations exercised upon women and intellectuals under the Islamic Regime in Iran where Nafisi taught literature to university students, she "dreamt of creating a special class, one that would give me the freedoms denied me in the classes I taught in the Islamic Republic" (p. 10). She began her memoir by offering a sketch of the community of women she assembled every Thursday in her living room in Tehran in fall 1995.

> I have the two photographs in front of me now. In the first there are seven women, standing against a white wall. They are, according to the law of the land, dressed in black robes and head scarves, covered except for the oval of their faces and their hands. In the second photograph the same group, in the same position, stands against the same wall. Only they have taken off their coverings. Splashes of color separate one from the next. Each has become distinct through the color and style of her clothes, the color and the length of her hair; not even the two who are still wearing their head scarves look the same. (p. 4)
>
> For nearly two years, almost every Thursday morning, rain or shine, they came to my house, and almost every time, I could not get over the shock of seeing them shed their mandatory veils and robes and burst into color. When my students came into that room, they took off more than their scarves and robes. Gradually, each one gained an outline and a shape, becoming her own inimitable self. Our world in that living room with its window framing my beloved Elburz Mountains became our sanctuary, our self-contained universe, mocking the reality of black-scarved, timid faces in the city that sprawled below. (pp. 5–6)

I read Nafisi's memoir as a testament to the ways women's desires are molded and manipulated when women find themselves living in a situation where they have limited to no control. In gathering her students in her living room, Nafisi provided a space for her female students to explore alternative conceptions and possibilities for themselves. She "formulated certain general questions for [her students] to consider, the most central of which was how these great works of imagination could help us in our present trapped situation as women" (p. 19). Reminiscent of Beauvoir's analysis of the Marquis de Sade, which was discussed in chapter 3, Nafisi continually reminds us that to inscribe one's own desires on another person is the most harmful thing one can do. In the case of the Islamic Republic, Nafisi argues that the idea of woman became a static image. In light of this image, women were expected to behave in certain ways. Every single aspect of dress and behavior was to be regulated. Nafisi recalls, "The pressure was hardest on the students. I felt helpless as I listened to their endless tales of woe. Female students were being penalized for running up the stairs when they were late for classes, for laughing in the hallways, for talking to members of the opposite sex. One day Sanaz had barged into class near the end of the session, crying. In between bursts of tears, she explained that she was late because the female guards at the door, finding a blush in her bag, had tried to send her home with a reprimand" (p. 9).

Subject to controls, checks, and the watchful eyes of the censors, women become the outward symbol of the Revolution's success or failure—pawns in a power struggle between conflicting visions of Iranian culture. Nafisi astutely analyzes the way the image of woman was manipulated—for example in wearing the veil—in the battles between modernization, deemed as Westernization, and tradition, manifested in this case as Islamic culture. Nafisi elaborates, "From the beginning of the revolution there had been many aborted attempts to impose the veil on women; these attempts failed because of persistent and militant resistance put up mainly by Iranian women. In many important ways the veil had gained a symbolic significance for the regime. Its reimposition would signify the complete victory of the Islamic aspect of the revolution, which in those first years was not a foregone conclusion. The unveiling of women mandated by Reza Shah in 1936 had been a controversial symbol of modernization, a powerful sign of the reduction of the clergy's power. It was important for the ruling clerics to reassert that power. All this I can explain now, with the advantage of hindsight, but it was far from clear then" (p. 112).

Nafisi's insights complicate any simplistic reading of the veil. Numerous feminists have written on the complexities of the role of women within Islam and the reductionist logic implicit in equating the wearing of the veil with a limitation on freedom, and the refusal of the veil as a liberating act. The problem is not with wearing the veil itself—in fact some Islamic feminists wear the veil as a mark of urban educated sophistication[1]—but the imposition of a certain form of dress to symbolize propriety or piety for women, and the refusal of that same form of dress to symbolize liberation. What is fascinating in terms of the politics of the veil and the practice of veiling is that not only are there many forms of the practice but also that this particular mode of dress is implicated within a complex imperial and colonial context in which men, both from the West and within nationalist contexts, exert their power by exercising control over women's bodies. As Nancy Hirschmann (2003, 179) puts it, "Women's bodies become the physical spaces on which men construct their illusions of power and mastery over their own lives." Uma Narayan (1997) also writes of the way women's roles and female sexuality often become contested sites of representation in battles between Western and indigenous culture. Discussing the example of India, she argues that "veiling, polygamy, child-marriage, and *sati* were all significant points of conflict and negotiation between colonizing 'Western' culture and different colonized Third-World cultures" (p. 17). Indigenous and religious practices became a symbol of the backwardness of third-world cultures to which male-dominated, third-world elites responded by "constructing these very practices as sacred and longstanding traditions that were constitutive of their values and world views, and as practices that were tied to the spiritual place of, and respect for, women in their cultures" (ibid.). Referring again to the photographs of her students taken in her home, Nafisi poignantly expresses the lack of space women were given to discover who they might want to be outside of the battles over the image of woman. She claims, "The two photographs should be placed side by side. Both embody the 'fragile unreality' —to quote Nabakov on his own state of exile—of our existence in the Islamic Republic of Iran. One cancels the other, and yet without one, the other is incomplete. In the first photograph, standing there in our black robes and scarves, we are as we had been shaped by someone else's dreams. In the second, we appear as we imagined ourselves. In neither could we feel completely at home" (p. 24).

As indicated already, Nafisi, a Nabakov scholar, creatively read *Lolita* to signify what she found to be the most serious crimes against women under the Islamic Republic. Discussing one of her students named Yassi, Nafisi elaborates on why she found life in Iran under the ayatollahs to be so oppressive. She argues that though her students were from very different social, political, and religious contexts and often did not share common views on religion, for example, their dilemmas "were shared, and stemmed from the confiscation of their most intimate moments and private aspirations by the regime" (2003, 273). Nafisi observed of her students that "although they came from very different backgrounds, the regime that ruled them had tried to make their personal identities and histories irrelevant. They were never free of the regime's definition of them as Muslim women. Whoever we were—and it was not really important what religion we belonged to, whether we wished to wear the veil or not, whether we observed certain religious norms or not—we had become the figment of someone else's dreams" (p. 28). Inspired by reading *Lolita* with her students, Nafisi elaborates, "Take *Lolita*. This was the story of a twelve-year-old girl who had nowhere to go. Humbert had tried to turn her into his fantasy, into his dead love, and he had destroyed her. The desperate truth of *Lolita's* story is *not* the rape of a twelve-year-old by a dirty old man but *the confiscation of one individual's life by another*. We don't know what Lolita would have become if Humbert had not engulfed her. Yet the novel, the finished work, is hopeful, beautiful even, a defense not just of beauty but of life, ordinary everyday life, all the normal pleasures that Lolita, like Yassi, was deprived of" (p. 33). Nafisi continues, "Warming up and suddenly inspired, I added that in fact Nabokov had taken revenge against our own solipsizers; he had taken revenge on the Ayatollah Khomeini, on Yassi's last suitor, on the dough-faced teacher for that matter. They had tried to shape others according to their own dreams and desires, but Nabokov, through his portrayal of Humbert, had exposed all solipsists who take over other people's lives. She, Yassi, had much potential; she could be whatever she wanted to be—a good wife or a teacher and poet. What mattered was for her to know what she wanted" (ibid.).

Figuring out what one wants, however, can be a difficult process, just as the critical evaluation of choice becomes increasingly complex when we acknowledge that subjects and choices are constructed within contexts of power. Certainly women's ability to choose is key to women's freedom, yet choosing a particular practice does not itself make it a free action, or even a protest.[2] One of the aspects of the regime that Nafisi (2003) found most frightening is its ability to get people to willingly cooperate. As she articulated, "The worst crime committed by totalitarian mind-sets is that they force their citizens, including their victims, to become complicit in their crimes. Dancing with your jailer, participating in your own execution, that is an act of utmost brutality. My students witnessed it in show trials on television and enacted it every time they went out into the streets dressed as they were told to dress. They had not become part of the crowd who watched the executions, but they did not have the power to protest them, either" (p. 76).

Preserving "individuality, that unique quality which evades description but differentiates one human being from the other" (Nafisi 2003, 77), is the key, Nafisi claims, to discovering the self and one's desires. Against this, the jailors "invaded all private spaces and tried to shape every gesture, to force us to become one of them, and that in itself was another form of execution" (ibid.). I argue, however, that Nafisi articulated a more effective affront to the jailers. Rather than look to the individual, reinscribing a notion of the liberal self as able to be known autonomously and outside one's cultural and political context, Nafisi's efforts to create a community of women from radically different backgrounds and to bring them together in dialogue is the more subversive and potentially liberating move. Nafisi combined these two instincts in her love of literature read within a community of women. She wrote that preserving one's own consciousness and individuality—and recognizing it in others—is best expressed within certain works of great literature. Speaking of this aspect in Jane Austen's work, Nafisi observes, "One of the most wonderful things about *Pride and Prejudice* is the variety of voices it embodies. There are so many different forms of dialogue: between several people, between two people, internal dialogue and dialogue through letters....In Austen's novels, there are spaces for oppositions that do not need to eliminate each other in order to exist. There is also space—-not just space but a necessity—for self-reflection and self-criticism. Such reflection is the cause of change. We needed no message, no outright call for plurality, to prove our point. All we needed was to read and appreciate the cacophony of voices to understand its democratic imperative" (p. 268).

A community is created within Austen's literature, as in Nafisi's living room, where different voices are heard and appreciated. Just as Carolyn Steedman (1986, 16) desired to tell the story of her mother, an "inhabitant from the long streets," Nafisi (2003) brought us the stories of a few women students in the Islamic Republic. This all may sound a bit romantic. Feminists may legitimately question what women across cultures, class, and various ethnicities have in common. As we learned from Beauvoir, Nafisi's memoir reminds us that the most important thing is for women to speak and listen to each other—for women with diverse lived realities to tell the story of their lives in light of, and to inspire, feminist consciousness. Nafisi warned, however, that "we are all capable of becoming the blind censor, of imposing our visions and desires on others" (p. 315).

For women to resist a static image of femininity as well as for the feminist movement to resist becoming the blind censor, feminists must embrace genealogy, seeking out the stories of their mother's lives, as well as seeking the stories of women from marginalized communities. Gayatri Chakravorty Spivak questioned whether women whose lives are so different from each other can ever speak to and hear each other. She wondered, for example, how the metropolitan feminist might learn from and speak to the millions of illiterate rural and urban Indian women (Deutscher 2002, 182). In *But Enough about Me*, Nancy K. Miller (2002, 124) asked a similar question, inquiring as to why it is "so difficult to cross the borders of the self to identify with those not like us." She claimed, "Part of the problem resides in the disparity between those with an autobiography (the story of the proper name) and those with a collective, unauthored story" (p. 125). Steedman (1986, 16), for example, looked back on her working-class mother's life as a counterpoint to Beauvoir's upper-class story of her mother's death.

> The first task is to particularize this profoundly a-historical landscape (and so this book details a mother who was a working woman and a single parent, and a father who wasn't a patriarch). And once the landscape is detailed and historicized in this way, the urgent need becomes to find a way of theorizing the result of such difference and particularity, not in order to find a description that can be universally applied (the point is *not* to say that all working class childhoods are the same, nor that experience of them produces unique psychic structures) but so that the people in exile, the inhabitants of the long streets, may start to use the autobiographical "I," and tell the stories of their life.

But as Penelope Deutscher (2002) pointed out, Spivak questioned whether there ever can be real communication—even if the stories are told, even when a woman claims the autobiographical "I." As Deutscher put it, "transparency of understanding will not be achieved with good intentions and attentive listening…it is better to be attentive to the necessary limits of understanding, achieved through respect for the 'secret' that must escape the best efforts of the well-intentioned" (p. 182). The violation of dignity and the refusal to open up spaces for desire often occurs within our attempts at "multicultural, intracultural, and transnational dialogues between women" (Cornell 2002, xix) when, for example, some women and their needs come to stand in for all women, or when feminists "deny the dignity of the very women they are trying to help" by framing their interventions as a "rescue by enlightened Western feminist organizations" (ibid., 2). Writing about Afghan women under the Taliban, Lila Abu-Lughod (2002, 787) remarked that we must accept the possibility of difference: "Can we only free Afghan women to be like us or might we have to recognize that even after 'liberation' from the Taliban, they might want different things than we would want for them?" Yet we must be careful to avoid cultural relativism. Hirschmann (2003, 198) reminds us that the terms of "cultural difference" are "all too often defined by and in the interests of men who have political power."

Therefore, we must be ready to make critical comparisons and judgments in light of the different desires that various locations and contexts produce, while carving spaces for women to be able to create the conditions under which they choose and frame the choices themselves. In pressing for feminists to explore the genealogies of their literal and figurative mothers and to read these alongside those of their feminist peers, I do not claim that we can ever truly know another woman's story. The best we can do is to read what that woman has written or listen to what she says, with feminist consciousness of the material, historical, and social circumstances within which each woman lives and the struggles individual women must engage in to form coalitions that challenge malleable versions of the myth of being a woman. Steedman (1986) again reminded us of always keeping the particularity and specificity of every woman's life in mind as we seek to connect them within feminist genealogies. As she said, "Simone de Beauvoir wrote of her mother's death, said that in spite of the pain it was an easy one: an upper-class death. Outside for the poor, dying is a different matter. She [Steedman's mother] lived alone, she died alone: a working-class life, a working-class death" (p. 2).

Contextualizing her mother's desire for material comfort and giving voice to a desire that conforms with the politics of the Tory party in class-conscious Britain, Steedman (1986) demonstrated not only that "humans are social beings, always raised in certain social and historical contexts and belonging to particular communities that shape their desires and understandings of the world" (Abu-Lughod 2002, 786) but also that the condemnation of this desire for material goods by progressives and feminists as a form of false consciousness fails to capture the sense of freedom and longing Steedman's mother articulated within her class location. Her mother's particular desire and her mother's understanding of her relationship to social class and freedom was the psychological underpinning of Steedman's world. As we saw in chapter 1, in longing for some of the accoutrements of proper femininity (e.g., a full skirt, the prince who never came) Steedman's mother struggled with the demands of femininity in multiple ways with which Steedman as a daughter must reckon.

Genealogies, Legacies, and Feminist Consciousness

Mohanty (2003, 141) argues that she came to study the "common interests" of third-world women workers in light of her own struggle for "self-definition and autonomy outside the definitions of daughter, wife, and mother." Mohanty adds that the "fact of being women with particular racial, ethnic, cultural, sexual, and geographical histories has everything to do with our definitions and identities as workers" (p. 142). In *The Curious Feminist: Searching for Women in a New Age of Empire*, Cynthia Enloe (2004, 47) argues that around the globe (e.g., South Korea, Afghanistan, Iraq, Vietnam) "if women [were to] reimagine their lives as daughters, as wives, as workers, as citizens...it would shake the very foundations of the whole political system." Each woman's situation, to use Beauvoir's terminology, is profoundly different, yet women share the situation of struggling to redefine ways of being women within the demands of femininity specific to their location. In *Massacre of the Dreamers*, Ana Castillo (1995) moved beyond the autobiographical "I" to write not just of her own life but instead as an exemplar for Chicanas. She explains, "I have not always spoken from my personal experience because I know that unlike millions of women, I as a writer have a voice that can be heard. And this fact has marked my life as indisputably distinct from those who do not" (p. 205).

I explore Castillo's work next alongside a few selected sections of Lorde's (1982) *Zami: A New Spelling of My Name* and with a return to the call for genealogies in the work of Steedman (1986), Cornell (2002), and Narayan (1997) to emphasize the importance of raising consciousness within communities of radically different women to create the potential for coalitions and solidarity. Castillo (1995) is well aware of her privileged position with regard to the world's women. She is an educated professor and writer, someone who in her role as an intellectual will be noticed and heard. Because of these differences, she calls for solidarity. Castillo writes, "As Xicanistas [Chicanas with feminist consciousness, Xicanisma] who may or may not find ourselves in garment sweatshops in Los Angeles, earning seven cents a garment, or working in indentured servant conditions in the fields with our children for twelve hours a day, or in any number of other heinous labour conditions akin to feudalism that millions of women are forced to endure today, every day in order to feed our children—we must not forget our hermanas [sisters] who do" (p. 61).

To not forget our sisters and to stand in solidarity with them, we are called on to raise consciousness—*Xicanisma* as Castillo (1995) called it—concerning the conditions of life and the static images of femininity that serve to keep women—advantaged as well as disadvantaged—trapped within their situations. Castillo engaged in genealogical feminist work studying the struggles of her Latina mothers with Catholicism, conservative Mexican values that remain suspicious of female sexuality, and even Marxism and the male-dominated Chicano movement. Catholicism, for example, plays a significant role in the lives of Mexican women, influencing how they look at the world and how they feel about themselves. Castillo is especially interested in how Church doctrine views female sexuality as perverse; she argues that "the subordination of women's sexuality was crucial for the survival of patriarchal religious practices" (p. 107).

> Lesbian and heterosexual women alike grappled for many years with their Catholic indoctrination, which has adamantly repressed female desire. While heterosexual woman may not feel the Catholic Church controlling their sexual behavior as much as in the past, they are still conscious of a restrictive stance against the use of contraceptives and abortion, issues that directly affect their sexuality. The Mexican-Catholic lesbian, rejected by family and ostracized by her immediate community, may find it painful and even impossible to acknowledge a direct connection between her faith and the rejection she suffers as a woman who loves women because Catholicism is so much a part of her sense of self. (p. 139)

But it is not only Catholicism that subordinates women. Sounding much like Belli (2002) and Nafisi (2003) in their criticisms of revolutionary movements that fail to consider the reality of women's lives, Castillo takes the Chicano movement to task.

> The philosophy of the male-dominated Chicano Movement was akin to the theories of Frantz Fanon, who professed that revolutionary struggle for

"national independence" would suffice to change people's attitudes toward women's subordinate status. The participation of women in the national struggle would prove their equality to the men and at the same time change women so that they would demand their own "liberation." However, in the case of the Algerian revolution where the people freed themselves of 130 years of colonization in 1962 this indeed did not happen. Each struggle for national freedom must be evaluated in its own historical context but national struggles continue to disregard the reality that women ultimately remain subject to male authority. By male I do not restrict myself to actual men but to the system. (p. 53)

Like Goldman in her critique of her anarchist colleagues, and like Belli in her confronation with her Sandinista comrades, Castillo argues that the Chicano movement failed to live up to a feminist ideal of taking women's concerns seriously. She is scathingly critical of static images of woman, as they manifest themselves in Chicano and Chicana culture, to perpetuate stereotypes that serve to deny women their freedom. Yet also like Goldman and Belli, Castillo does not want to give up all aspects of the feminine. She looks, in fact, to preserve aspects of the feminine that she finds integral to women's lived realities. Though she is highly critical of the Catholic hierarchy, for example, she argues that Mexican women's worshipping of the Virgin is an "unspoken, if not unconscious, devotion to their own version of the Goddess" (p. 48). Turning to the cult of Guadelupe is an indication, as Castillo sees it, of the "need for spiritual consolation and material relief" (ibid.). Moreover, she argues that to abandon all of the traditional values associated with the feminine would fail to constitute feminist consciousness. The version of feminist conscious-ness called for by Castillo is quite innovative, especially in light of struggles with the demands of femininity that have been discussed throughout this book.

> With the tenacious insistence at integrating a feminist perspective to their
> political conscientización as Chicanas, feminist activistas, and intellectu-
> als are in the process of developing what I call Xicanisma. On a pragmatic
> level, the basic premise of Xicanisma is to reconsider behavior long seen as
> inherent in the Mexican Amerindian woman's character, such as, patience,
> perseverance, industriousness, loyalty to one's clan, and commitment to our
> children. Contrary to how those incognizant of what feminism is, we do
> not reject these virtues. We may not always welcome the taxing responsibil-
> ity that comes with our roles as Chicanas. We've witnessed what strain and
> limitations they often placed on our mothers and other relatives. But these
> traits often seen as negative and oppressive to our growth as women, as well
> as having been translated to being equal to being a drone for white society
> and its industrial interests, may be considered strengths. Simultaneously,
> as we redefine (not categorically reject) our roles within our families, com-
> munities at large, and white dominant society, our Xicanisma helps us to be
> self-confident and assertive regarding the pursuing of our needs and desires.
> (p. 40)

Key to Castillo's version of feminist consciousness is the need to redefine, rather than to completely reject, women's roles. Though she failed
to specify exactly what this would mean, especially how the feminine
solidifies in stereotypes of femininity and how we can keep it from doing
so, I understand Castillo's project to be one that involves an expansion
of the meanings given to being a woman without in any way conflating
this with dominant masculinity (Halberstam's [2002] elite masculinity) or necessarily rejecting everything the feminine has stood for in the
past. Castillo, in my view, wants to open up a space for the feminine,
and offer possibilities for new ways to be a woman, beyond the choices
between copying masculinity or succumbing to femininity.

Cornell (2002) also contributes to theorizing how to make space
for women's desires. She seeks to restore what she calls the "dignity"
of women by allowing women to express their desire outside an

economy of the same in which only dominant norms of femininity can be witnessed and enacted. Cornell's definition of dignity seeks to make space for women to realize their freedom: "dignity is a claim on ourselves that signals a world that might be faithful to our freedom" (p. 2). Speculating on how we might generate and articulate this claim for dignity Cornell adds, "Our dignity and the demand for its respect stem from actual resistance, but also from the broken dreams that are turned into hopes for our daughters. Dignity inheres in evaluations we all have to make of our lives, the ethical decisions we consciously confront, and even the ones we ignore" (p. xix). I read Cornell as engaging in the kind of work on feminist genealogy that might inspire feminists to articulate links between women's lives. In this way, we might illuminate our common struggles, forge communities of solidarity with other women, and muster the strength to avoid living in accordance to what femininity requires of us in our specific locations.

Cornell (2002) argues that though dignity is not something we can lose, it can be violated and often is. This is witnessed by intergenerational rage and resentment between generations of women. In "giving advice about how to survive" (p. xix) within patriarchal structures, women often violate the dignity of their daughters. In chapter 1, I spoke of Narayan's (1997) admonishment to her mother about the injunction to remain silent and to become a good Indian woman. Lorde (1982) experienced something similar with her own mother. In *Zami*, Lorde wrote of the ways her mother tried to shield her from the pain of being black. Any racist incident was dismissed as an anomaly or an unforeseen accident. Lorde's mother took pains, Lorde wrote, "to hide from us as children the many instances of her powerlessness" (p. 17). She either worked to change reality, or she changed her perception of it, acting as if the repeated humiliations their family endured (e.g., suffering a "nasty glob of grey spittle" on a coat or shoe) were "totally random" (Lorde 1982, 18). Lorde was left completely unprepared for the racism she would have to endure in her life. She tells one particularly poignant story of how, promised by her teacher that the smartest girl would be elected class president, Lorde went against her mother's strict instructions and ran for the office. When the most popular girl at school won, Lorde was met by her mother's humiliation and anger: "Through my tears, I saw my mother's face stiffen with rage. Her eyebrows drew together as her hand came up, still holding her handbag. I stopped in my tracks as her first blow caught me full on the side of my head. My mother was no weakling, and I backed away, my ears ringing. The whole world seemed to be going insane. It was only then that I remembered our earlier conversations" (p. 64).

Cornell (2002, 19) also witnessed this dynamic in exploring the relationship between her grandmother and her mother: "My grandmother's concern for the protection of my space for imagination and self-expression seemed to operate exactly opposite to the way in which she constrained my mother." Cornell said she could only speculate about why this was the case, which was especially odd since her grandmother was an unconventional woman who lived beyond the norms of femininity. She speculated, "My grandmother was haunted by the fear that the freedom she claimed for herself could somehow lead her to be punished by society—a society that could take her daughter away from her" (ibid.). Cornell's mother, until the end of her life, mostly lived as a proper woman. Early on, however, Cornell said her mother may have tried to resist some norms of femininity. She had, for example, told Cornell's father that she might not want children. He responded by suggesting that she see a psychiatrist (p. 21). Steedman's (1986, 69) mother, in contrast, had children willingly but as a political act in which she saw herself as both "bargain and bargainer." Steedman wrote that her mother saw her children as levers to get what she wanted, and she "exchanged herself for a future" (ibid.). As Steedman saw it, her mother made a conscious choice: a "bargain struck between working-class women and the state, the traffic being a baby and the bargain itself freedom, autonomy, state benefits, and a council house: the means of subsistence" (p. 70). Like Beauvoir's mother, Steedman's and Cornell's mothers could never articulate their desire.

Cornell wrote of her mother's desire as it manifested itself in another way: giving birth to her book on genealogies. Cornell's mother desired to have her daughter, Cornell, write a book that would bear witness to the dignity of her death. *Legacies of Dignity: Between Women and Generations* is the enactment of Cornell's promise to her mother to write such a book. We learn in the first line that suffering from multiple ailments, Cornell's mother decided to take her own life. This is not, however, a book about the right to die with dignity within the legal, juridical realm. It is instead an attempt to attest to her mother's dignity by opening up the space for her mother's desire as a struggle with the demands of femininity. Cornell did not say it in those words, but as with Steedman's memoir, I find that this memoir exemplifies the quest to express the mother's—indeed, any woman's—desire beyond the expectations for women within the constraints of femininity. Both Cornell and Steedman, like Beauvoir before them, attempted to map women's—in this case their mother's—desire within a context that opens up space for women beyond norms of femininity.

Cornell (2002, 27) adds that her daughter, Sarita Graciela Kellow Cornell, a Latina adopted from Paraguay, will inherit the story Cornell told as "the struggle to represent the gaps and silences in my mother and grandmother's relationship." The story Cornell told of her grandmother and mother is by necessity a partial and limited one. Cornell made no claim to fully or completely understand their desires; what she sought instead is the necessity of telling something about them that will represent their struggles with the demands of femininity and show the necessity of carving a space for the "feminine within the imaginary domain" (p. 31). Cornell elaborated, "The radicalism of my argument follows from the claim that the more we actively assume our desire, the less we are captured by traditional gender roles, and are thus enabled to assume our 'special responsibility' for our lives. By desire, I do not mean simply sexual desire, but rather what we broadly conceive as our ability to chart out a life that is our own" (ibid.).

To be able to make critical comparisons that truly can attend to situation and context, feminists must open up spaces for dialogue. Cornell's (2002) work on genealogy attempts to do just that. Writing about her mother, her grandmother, her daughter, and the immigrant women in the housecleaner's *Unity* labor collective, Cornell's work links stories and encounters among different women and different generations without specifying what feminist freedom will substantively contain. Though these women with whom we connect and share stories can never be fully known, each must be free to be a subject of her own desire. We are called to respect the dignity of other women within and among our differences to break out of our roles, theorized by Beauvoir as the inessential and as man's Other.

Whereas Castillo (1995) called for a revolutionary feminist consciousness steeped in the traditions and context of Chicana feminism and unwilling to abandon what she called a feminine principle, Lorde warned against a naive invocation of sisterhood. The focus on solidarity beyond sisterhood calls on us to acknowledge that in spite of distinct conditions of oppression, we cannot turn our backs on the reality that women share much in common. We simply cannot abandon the universal call for solidarity despite the many differences in situation women experience. If we recognize these commonalities in our attempts to become women differently, outside the demands of femininity, we might forge political coalitions based in an enhanced feminist consciousness.

Conclusion

Beyond Femininity

When a feminist embraces the mark of sexual difference and speaks as a woman, the move is laden with personal ambivalence and political risk. Beauvoir's (1989, xix) first two lines of *The Second Sex* speak precisely to this point: "For a long time I have hesitated to write a book on woman. The subject is irritating, especially to women; and it is not new." Reckoning with the fraught notion of what it means to be a woman has been integral to the feminist movement since the second wave. To be named as a woman signifies a lack of freedom. For feminism to speak in the name of women as a category was revealed as exclusionary. Therefore, when feminists identify as women, there is the danger that making any descriptive claims about women will further entrench women in our otherness and that speaking categorically as women can never represent all varieties of women. Thus, many contemporary feminists have argued that claims that feminism could speak in the name of women were never and will never be possible. Modern feminism has been steeped in the paradoxical position of needing both to accept and to refuse sexual difference to continue as a political movement.

The relationship between women and femininity is central to Beauvoir's (1989) project, as I articulate throughout this book. She wrote, "All agree in recognizing the fact that females exist in the human species; today as always they make up about one half of human-ity. And yet we are told that femininity is in danger; we are exhorted to be women, remain women, become women. It would appear, then, that every female human being is not necessarily a woman; to be so considered she must share in that mysterious and threatened reality known as femininity. Is this attribute something secreted by the ovaries? Or is it a Platonic essence, a product of the philosophi-cal imagination? Is a rustling petticoat enough to bring it down to earth?" (p. xix). Proceeding to describe femininity as an essence, or as an unchangeably fixed entity labeled the eternal feminine, Beauvoir argued that it never truly existed. The idea of the eternal feminine was, she concluded, a result of how "men have fancied her [woman] in their dreams" (p. 138), combined with characteristics exhibited by real women "as a reaction dependent in part upon a situation" (p. xx). Whereas Beauvoir identified the eternal feminine to dispute its exis-tence through the details of women's lives, I instead describe feminin-ity itself as a situation—one with which all women must contend. As I demonstrate throughout this book, femininity is an ever-malleable construct, adapted to the contexts and locations in which women live out their lives. To live and struggle with the demands of femininity defines the situation in which feminists seek to create their lives in more expansive and fulfilling ways, with an enhanced scope to how they might live as women.

As we also see, these feminists mostly had to struggle alone, even while recognizing and writing about the common struggles all women face. Feminists such as Mary Wollstonecraft, Germaine de Staël, Ida B. Wells, Emma Goldman, and Simone de Beauvoir were fully aware of the way that being named as a woman marked them as belonging to an oppressed group. Yet though conscious of being women with other women, when these individual women attempted to live their lives outside of gender expectations they felt isolated from other women in their attempts to live differently. Beauvoir reminded us that women are always embedded within their situations, and often the alliances women feel with class, race, and emotional and familial attachments—particularly with men—make it difficult for women to act together politically. In other words, the manifestations of femininity make it very difficult for women to act politically specifically as women. Women act politically all the time yet within other kinds of coalitions and under different types of identity umbrellas under which they see themselves as belonging.

Yet for feminism to move forward, women must struggle together. Placing the work of historical feminist thinkers alongside contemporary feminists such as Carolyn Steedman, Audre Lorde, Uma Narayan, Gioconda Belli, Azar Nafisi, Ana Castillo, and Drucilla Cornell, I chart the common struggles women encounter, played out both in isolated as well as collective ways, to encourage consciousness of the role femininity plays in women's lives. I suggest that this consciousness, born through recognition of the conditions of women's lives—particularly of our mothers and feminist mothers—could lead to political alliances among all kinds of women across identity categories.

For feminists to act within coalition does not necessarily mean that women must agree on goals designated as women's interests, nor must we specify the substantive end for which women are fighting. Feminism's collective effort to specify who women are and what women want has curtailed our efforts to forge ourselves as a political group open to contestation about who belongs and what we might need. Zerilli (2005, 171) writes of this tension, remarking that "feminists have not adequately articulated the difference between speaking about women as a demographic or social group and speaking about women as a political collectivity." Reconstituting the idea of a universal category, Zerilli contends that the universal need not be constructed by subsuming particulars under rules but rather could be a process of "making claims in a political space" that is "constituted through the very practice of making such claims" (p. 173).

I argue that political coalitions and the political claims they might engender could spring from a common recognition on the part of women that our desires for freedom are limited by the constraints of femininity. One contribution this book makes to these debates about articulating the vexed relationship between femininity and women, or as Zerilli (2005) put it differently, between women as a demographic and women as a potential political collectivity, is my focus on the changing manifestations of femininity and their impact on even the freest-thinking feminists. I show throughout that femininity is a force with which women constantly must reckon, even when they are consciously striving to break free of conventional gender norms. Femininity differently constrains and enables all women's lives. To recognize its impact within various histories, cultures, and identity categories encourages feminists to think politically about how we are called to be women, how we might articulate ourselves as women within coalition, and how we might move beyond the confines of this designation together. The commonalities I have discovered within the lives and work of these feminists do not point to similarity in the particulars of their situation or to identity features such as race, class, sexuality, age, or ability. What these women do have in common is that they were and are subject to the varying demands of femininity. The social meanings ascribed to being women, embedded within historical and material circumstances, differently affects all women.

Each thinker I study in this book is shown to have struggled with the particular meanings of femininity—how they were constructed as a demographic or a social group—while desiring at the same time to preserve aspects of the feminine that they consider integral to their sense of self. I demonstrate that though being a woman is laden with personal ambivalence and social and political exclusion, not one of the women whose life and work I explore in this book was willing or desired to live her life as a man. On the contrary, they wanted to live their lives as women, but with an enhanced sense of freedom and possibility and an enlarged scope given to the meanings associated with who a woman might become. I describe this dynamic for each thinker as conducting existential experiments with the feminine within the material conditions that structure women's lives.

Identifying as women, beyond femininity, as participants in a shared existential struggle to create meaning outside of the norms of gender, is the key moment in recognizing the possibility for political action. To see oneself as within a feminist genealogy, in our relationships with our mothers of all kinds and with other women, is the important step toward the feminist consciousness needed to be able to see the possibility of forming political coalitions with and as women. Opening up space for women's desire beyond the demands of femininity entails rereading the stories of women's lives—our mothers' lives—in ways that challenge the familiar patriarchal family plot (i.e., heterosexual sexuality, a desire for children, the assumption of the nuclear family, and the gender roles that inscribe it). Lorde (1982, 7) called this a movement from the "age-old triangle of mother father and child" to the "elegantly strong triad of grandmother mother daughter."

My work with these feminist thinkers more deeply illuminates the epigraph I placed at the beginning of the preface. The Milan Women's Bookstore Collective (1987, 138) observed that "a woman is free when she chooses to signify her belonging to the female sex, well knowing it is not an object of choice." By way of a focus on the demands of femininity, throughout this book I offer an alternative way to bring women together in political coalition without needing to make any essential statements about who women are, who women might become, or what women want. By reading the stories and sharing the contexts and situations of each other's lives, I hope to open a space for all of us to become women differently.

Bibliography

Abu-Lughod, Lila. 2002. Do Muslim Women Really Need Saving? Anthropological Reflections on Cultural Relativism and Its Others. *American Anthropologist* 104, no. 3:783–90.

Ackelsberg, Martha. 1991. *Free Women of Spain: Anarchism and the Struggle for the Emancipation of Women*. Bloomington: Indiana University Press.

Arendt, Hannah. 1965. *On Revolution*. New York: Viking.

———. 1982. *Lectures on Kant's Political Philosophy*, ed. Ronald Beiner. Chicago, IL: University of Chicago Press.

———. 1997. *Rahel Varnhagen: The Life of a Jewess*, ed. Liliane Weissberg. Trans. Richard and Clara Winston. Baltimore, MD: Johns Hopkins University Press.

Arp, Kristana. 1995. Beauvoir's Concept of Bodily Alienation. In *Feminist Interpretations of Simone de Beauvoir*, ed. Margaret A. Simons, 161–77. University Park: Pennsylvania State University Press.

Barkley Brown, Elsa. 1997. What Has Happened Here: The Politics of Difference in Women's History and Feminist Politics. In *The Second Wave: A Reader in Feminist Theory*, ed. Linda Nicholson, 272–87. New York: Routledge Press.

Barnes, Hazel. 1998. Self-Encounter in *She Came to Stay*. In *Simone de Beauvoir: A Critical Reader*, ed. Elizabeth Fallaize 1, 57–82. London, UK: Routledge.

Battersby, Christine. 1989. *Gender and Genius: Towards a Feminist Aesthetics*. London, UK: Women's Press.

Bauer, Nancy. 2001. *Simone de Beauvoir, Philosophy, and Feminism*. New York: Columbia University Press.

Beauvoir, Simone de. 1953. Must We Burn Sade? In *The Marquis De Sade: Selections from His Writings and a Study by Simone de Beauvoir*. New York: Grove Press.

———. 1965. *A Very Easy Death*. New York: Pantheon.

———. 1976. *The Ethics of Ambiguity*. New York: Citadel Press.

———. 1982. *She Came to Stay*. London, UK: Fontana Paperbacks.

———. 1984. *The Prime of Life*. New York: Penguin.

———. 1986. *Memoirs of a Dutiful Daughter*. New York: Penguin.

———. 1989. *The Second Sex*. Trans. H. Parshley. New York: Vintage.

———. 1998. *A Transatlantic Love Affair: Letters to Nelson Algren*. New York: New Press.

———. 2004. *Simone de Beauvoir: Philosophical Writings*, ed. Margaret A. Simons. Urbana: University of Illinois Press.

Belli, Gioconda. 2002. *The Country under My Skin: A Memoir of Love and War*. New York: Alfred A. Knopf.

Bergoffen, Debra. 1997. *The Philosophy of Simone de Beauvoir: Gendered Phenomenologies, Erotic Generosities*. Albany: State University of New York Press.

Berlant, Lauren. 2000. Intimacy: A Special Issue. In *Intimacy*, ed. Lauren Berlant, 1–9. Chicago, IL: University of Chicago Press.

Braidotti, Rosi. 1989. The Politics of Ontological Difference. In *Between Feminism and Psychoanalysis*, ed. Teresa Brennan, 89–105. London, UK: Routledge.

———. 1994. *Nomadic Subjects: Embodiment and Sexual Difference in Contemporary Feminist Theory*. New York: Columbia.

Bromwich, David. 1995. Wollstonecraft as a Critic of Burke. *Political Theory* 23, no. 4:617–34.

Burke, Carolyn, Naomi Schor, and Margaret Whitford, eds. 1994. *Engaging with Irigaray*. New York: Columbia University Press.

Burke, Edmund. 1986. *Reflections on the Revolution in France*. New York: Penguin.

Butler, Judith. 1990. *Gender Trouble: Feminism and the Subversion of Identity*. New York: Routledge.

———. 1993. *Bodies that Matter: On the Discursive Limits of "Sex."* New York: Routledge.

———. 2004. *Undoing Gender*. New York: Routledge.

Cady Stanton, Elizabeth. 1993. *Eighty Years and More: Reminiscences, 1815–1897*. Boston, MA: Northeastern University Press.

Castillo, Ana. 1994. *So Far from God*. New York: Penguin.

———. 1995. *Massacre of the Dreamers: Essays on Xicanisma*. New York: Penguin.

Colwill, Elizabeth. 1989. Just Another *Citoyenne*? Marie-Antoinette on Trial, 1790–1793. *History Workshop Journal* 28:63–87.

Cook, Blanche Weisen. 1977. Female Support Networks and Political Activism: Lillian Wald, Crystal Eastman, Emma Goldman. *Chrysalis* 3:43–61.

Cornell, Drucilla. 1998. *At the Heart of Freedom: Feminism, Sex, and Equality*. Princeton, NJ: Princeton University Press.

———. 2002. *Legacies of Dignity: Between Women and Generations*. New York: Palgrave.

Cott, Nancy. 1987. *The Grounding of Modern Feminism*. New Haven, CT: Yale University Press.

Davis, Angela. 1981. *Women, Race, and Class*. New York: Vintage.

De Lauretis, Teresa. 1994. *The Practice of Love: Lesbian Sexuality and Perverse Desire*. Bloomington: Indiana University Press.

Deutscher, Penelope. 2002. *A Politics of Impossible Difference: The Later Work of Luce Irigaray*. Ithaca, NY: Cornell University Press.

Drinnon, Richard. 1961. *Rebel in Paradise: A Biography of Emma Goldman*. New York: Harper and Row.

DuBois, E., and Linda Gordon. 1983. Danger and Pleasure in Nineteenth Century Feminist Sexual Thought. *Feminist Studies* 9, no. 1:7–25.

Enloe, Cynthia. 2004. *The Curious Feminist: Searching for Women in a New Age of Empire*. Berkeley: University of California Press.

Evans, Sara. 1997. *Born for Liberty: A History of Women in America*. New York: Free Press.

Falco, Maria J., ed. 1996. *Feminist Interpretations of Mary Wollstonecraft*. University Park: Pennsylvania State Press.

Falk, Candace. 1990. *Love, Anarchy, and Emma Goldman: A Biography*. New Brunswick, NJ: Rutgers University Press.

Favret, Mary. 1993. *Romantic Correspondence: Women, Politics, and the Fiction of Letters*. Cambridge, UK: Cambridge University Press.

Ferguson, Ann. 1995. Feminist Communities and Moral Revolution. In *Feminism and Community*, ed. Penny Weiss, 367–97. Philadelphia, PA: Temple University Press.

Ferguson, Kathy. 2002. E.G.: Emma Goldman, for Example. Paper presented at the annual meeting of the American Political Science Association. September, Boston, MA.

Fraisse, Geneviève. 1994. *Reason's Muse: Sexual Difference and the Birth of Democracy*, trans. Jane Marie Todd. Chicago, IL: University of Chicago Press.

Gay Levy, Darline, and Harriet B. Applewhite. 1992. Women and Militant Citizenship in Revolutionary Paris. In *Rebel Daughters: Women and the French Revolution*, eds. Sara E. Melzer and Leslie W. Rabine, 79–101. New York: Oxford University Press.

Giddings, Paula. 1984. *When and Where I Enter: The Impact of Black Women on Race and Sex in America*. New York: Quill William Morrow.

Glassgold, P. 2001. *Anarchy: An Anthology of Emma Goldman's Mother Earth*. Washington, DC: Counterpoint.

Godineau, Dominique. 1998. *The Women of Paris and Their French Revolution*, trans. Katherine Streip. Berkeley: University of California Press.

Godwin, William. 1987. *Memoirs of the Author of "The Rights of Woman,"* ed. Richard Holmes. New York: Penguin.

Goldman, Emma. 1969a. Anarchism: What It Really Stands For. In *Anarchism and Other Essays*, 47–77. New York: Dover.

———. 1969b. The Drama: A Powerful Disseminator of Radical Thought. In *Anarchism and Other Essays*, 241–71. New York: Dover.

———. 1969c. Marriage and Love. In *Anarchism and Other Essays*, 227–39. New York: Dover.

———. 1969d. The Traffic in Women. In *Anarchism and Other Essays*, 177–94. New York: Dover.

———. 1969e. The Tragedy of Women's Emancipation. In *Anarchism and Other Essays*, 213–25. New York: Dover.

———. 1969f. Woman Suffrage. In *Anarchism and Other Essays*, 195–211. New York: Dover.

———. 1970a. *My Disillusionment in Russia*. New York: Thomas Crowell.

———. 1970b. *Living My Life*, vol. 1. New York: Dover.

———. 1970c. *Living My Life*, vol. 2. New York: Dover.

———. 1975. *Nowhere at Home: Letters from Exile of Emma Goldman and Alexander Berkman*, eds. R. Drinnon and A. Drinnon. New York: Schocken Books.

———. 1981. Mary Wollstonecraft, Her Tragic Life, and her Passionate Struggle for Freedom, ed. A. Wexler. *Feminist Studies* 7, no. 1:112–33.

———. 1987. *The Social Significance of Modern Drama*. London, UK: Applause Theatre Books.

———. 1998. Jealousy: Causes and a Possible Cure. In *Red Emma Speaks: An Emma Goldman Reader*, ed. A. Kates Shulman, 214–21. Amherst, MA: Humanity Books.

———. 2001. Letters to Ben Reitman, 1909, 1919. In *Women and Romance: A Reader*, ed. S. Ostrov Weisser, 97–101. New York: New York University Press.

Goodison, L. 2001. Really Being in Love Means Wanting to Live in a Different World. In *Women and Romance: A Reader*, ed. S. Ostrov Weisser, 157–72. New York: New York University Press.

Goodman, Dena. 1994. *The Republic of Letters: A Cultural History of the French Enlightenment*. Ithaca, NY: Cornell University Press.

Gothlin, Eva. Simone de Beauvoir's Notions of Appeal, Desire, and Ambiguity and Their Relationship to Jean-Paul Sartre's Notions of Appeal and Desire. In *The Philosophy of Simone de Beauvoir*, ed. Margaret A. Simons, *Hypatia* 14, no. 4:83–95.

Gunther-Canada, Wendy. 1996. Mary Wollstonecraft's "Wild Wish": Confounding Sex in the Discourse on Political Rights. In *Feminist Interpretations of Mary Wollstonecraft*, ed. Maria J. Falco, 61–83. University Park: Pennsylvania State University Press.

———. 1998. The Politics of Sense and Sensibility: Mary Wollstonecraft and Catharine Macaulay Graham on Burke's *Reflections on the Revolution in France*. In *Women Writers and the Early Modern British Political Tradition*, ed. Hilda L. Smith, 127–47. Cambridge, UK: Cambridge University Press.

———. 2001. *Rebel Writer: Mary Wollstonecraft and Enlightenment Politics*. Dekalb: Northern Illinois University Press.

Gurstein, R. 2002. Emma Goldman and the Tragedy of Modern Love. *Salmagundi*: 67–89.

Gutwirth, Madelyn. 1992. *Twilight of the Goddesses: Women and Representation in the French Revolutionary Era*. New Brunswick, NJ: Rutgers University Press.

———, Avriel Goldberger, and Karyna Szmurlo, eds. 1991. *Germaine de Staël: Crossing the Borders*. New Brunswick, NJ: Rutgers University Press.

Halberstam, Judith. 2002. An Introduction to Female Masculinity: Masculinity without Men. In *The Masculinity Studies Reader*, eds. Rachel Adams and David Savran, 355–74. London, UK: Blackwell.

Hawkesworth, Mary. 2004. The Semiotics of Premature Burial: Feminism in a Postfeminist Age. *SIGNS* 29, no. 4:961–86.

Hawthorne, Melanie C. 2000. *Contingent Loves: Simone de Beauvoir and Sexuality*. Charlottesville: University of Virginia Press.

Herold, J. Christopher. 1963. *The Age of Napoleon*. Boston, MA: Houghton Mifflin Company.

Hesse, Carla. 2001. *The Other Enlightenment: How French Women Became Modern*. Princeton, NJ: Princeton University Press.

Hirschmann, Nancy J. 2003. *The Subject of Liberty: Toward a Feminist Theory of Freedom*. Princeton, NJ: Princeton University Press.

Hooks, Bell. 1981. *"Ain't I a Woman?": Black Women and Feminism*. Boston, MA: South End Press.

Hunt, Lynn. 1991. The Many Bodies of Marie-Antoinette: Political Pornography and the Problem of the Feminine in the French Revolution. In *Eroticism and the Body Politic*, ed. Lynn Hunt, 108–30. Baltimore, MD: Johns Hopkins University Press.

Isbell, John. 1996. The Painful Birth of the Romantic Heroine: Staël as Political Animal, 1786–1818. *Romantic Review* 87:59–67.

Irigaray, Luce. 1985. *This Sex which Is Not One*, trans. Catherine Porter. Ithaca, NY: Cornell University Press.

———. 1990. Women's Exile: Interview with Luce Irigaray, trans. Couze Venn. In *The Feminist Critique of Language: A Reader,* ed. Deborah Cameron, 80–96. New York: Routledge.

———. 1993a. Body against Body: In Relation to the Mother. In *Sexes and Genealogies,* ed and trans. Gillian C. Gill, 7–21. New York: Columbia University Press.

———. 1993b. *An Ethics of Sexual Difference*, trans. Carolyn Burke and Gillian C. Gill. Ithaca, NY: Cornell University Press.

———. 1993c. *Je, Tu, Nous: Toward a Culture of Difference*, trans. Alison Martin. New York: Routledge.

Jackson, Stevi. 2001. Love and Romance as Objects of Feminist Knowledge. In *Women and Romance: A Reader*, ed. S. Ostrov Weisser, 254–64. New York: New York University Press.

Jacobus, Mary. 1995. *First Things: The Maternal Imaginary in Literature, Art, and Psychoanalysis*. New York: Routledge.

Katz, J. 1992, Almeda Sperry to Emma Goldman: Letters. In *Gay American History: Lesbians and Gay Men in the U.S.A.*, ed. J. Katz, 523–29. New York: Penguin.

Kelly, Gary. 1996. *Revolutionary Feminism: The Mind and Career of Mary Wollstonecraft*. London, UK: Macmillan.

Kollantai, A. 1972. Sexual Relations and the Class Struggle and Love and the New Morality, trans. and introd. Alix Holt Montpelier, 1–13 and 15–26. Bristol, CT: Falling Wall Press.

Kristeva, Julia. 1995. Glory, Grief, and Writing (A Letter to a "Romantic" Concerning Madame de Staël). In *New Maladies of the Soul*, trans. Ross Guberman, 159–71. New York: Columbia University Press.

Kruks, Sonia. 1987. Simone de Beauvoir and the Limits to Freedom. *Social Text* 17: 111–22.

———. 1995. Simone de Beauvoir: Teaching Sartre about Freedom. In *Feminist Interpretations of Simone de Beauvoir*, ed. Margaret A. Simons, 79–95. University Park: Pennsylvania State University Press.

———. 2001. *Retrieving Experience: Subjectivity and Recognition in Feminist Politics*. Ithaca, NY: Cornell University Press.

Landes, Joan. 1995. *Novus Ordo Saeclorum*: Gender and Public Space in Arendt's Revolutionary France. In *Feminist Interpretations of Hannah Arendt*, ed. Bonnie Honig, 195–215. University Park: Pennsylvania State University Press.

Lawrence, Karen R. 1994. *Penelope Voyages: Women and Travel in the British Literary Tradition*. Ithaca, NY: Cornell University Press.

Le Doeuff, Michèle. 2000. Beauvoir and Feminism. In *French Feminism Reader*, ed. Kelly Oliver, 35–57. New York: Rowman and Littlefield.

Lorde, Audre. 1982. *Zami: A New Spelling of My Name: A Biomythography by Audre Lorde*. Freedom, CA: Crossing Press.

———. 1984. *Sister Outsider*. Freedom, CA: Crossing Press.

Lundgren-Gothlin, Eva. 1996. *Sex and Existence: Simone de Beauvoir's "The Second Sex."* Hanover, NH: Wesleyan University Press.

Marks, Elaine. 1973. *Simone de Beauvoir: Encounters with Death*. New Brunswick, NJ: Rutgers University Press.

Marsh, M. 1981. *Anarchist Women, 1870–1920*. Philadelphia, PA: Temple University Press.

Marso, Lori Jo. 1999. *(Un)Manly Citizens: J. J. Rousseau's and Germaine de Staël's Subversive Women*. Baltimore, MD: Johns Hopkins University Press.

———. 2002. Defending the Queen: Wollstonecraft and Staël on the Politics of Sensibility and Feminine Difference. *Eighteenth-Century: Theory and Interpretation* 43, no. 1:43–60.

————, and Patricia Moynagh, eds. 2006. *Simone de Beauvoir's Political Thinking.* Urbana: University of Illinois Press.

Mellor, Anne K. 1993. *Romanticism and Gender.* London, UK: Routledge.

Meyer Spacks, Patricia. 1980. Selves in Hiding. In *Women's Autobiography: Essays in Criticism,* ed. E. Jelinek, 112–32. Bloomington: Indiana University Press.

Milan Women's Bookstore Collective. 1990. *Sexual Difference: A Theory of Social– Symbolic Practice.* Bloomington: Indiana University Press.

Miller, Nancy K. 1991. *Getting Personal: Feminist Occasions and Other Autobiographical Acts.* New York: Routledge.

————. 1997. Public Statements, Private Lives: Academic Memoirs for the Nineties. *SIGNS* 22, no. 4:981–1015.

————. 2002. *But Enough about Me: Why We Read Other People's Lives.* New York: Columbia University Press.

Mills, Sara. 1991. *Discourses of Difference: An Analysis of Women's Travel Writing and Colonialism.* London, UK: Routledge.

Mini, Anne A. A. 1995. *An Expressive Revolution: The Political Theory of Germaine de Staël.* Ph.D. diss., University of Washington.

Moi, Toril. 1994. *Simone de Beauvoir: The Making of an Intellectual Woman.* Oxford, UK: Blackwell.

————. 1999. *What Is a Woman?* Oxford, UK: Oxford University Press.

Mohanty, Chandra Talpade. 2004. *Feminism without Borders: Decolonizing Theory, Practicing Solidarity.* Durham, NC: Duke University Press.

Morton, M. 1992. *Emma Goldman and the American Left: Nowhere at Home.* New York: Twayne.

Moskal, Jeanne. 1991. The Picturesque and the Affectionate in Wollstonecraft's Letter from Norway. *Modern Language Quarterly* 52:263–94.

Moynagh, Patricia. 2006. Beauvoir on Lived Reality, Exemplary Validity, and a Method for Political Thought. In *Simone de Beauvoir's Political Thinking,* eds. Lori Jo Marso and Patricia Moynagh, 11–30. Urbana: University of Illinois Press.

Muraro, Luisa. 1994. Female Genealogies. In *Engaging with Irigaray,* eds. Carolyn Burke, Naomi Schor, and Margaret Whitford, 317–33. New York: Columbia University Press.

Myers, Mitzi. 1979. Mary Wollstonecraft's Letters Written…in Sweden: Toward Romantic Autobiography. *Studies in Eighteenth-Century Culture* 8:65–185.

————. 1981. Godwin's *Memoirs* of Wollstonecraft: The Shaping of Self and Subject. *SiR* 20:299–316.

Nafisi, Azar. 2003. *Reading Lolita in Tehran: A Memoir in Books.* New York: Random House.

Narayan, Uma. 1997. *Dislocating Cultures: Identities, Traditions, and Third-World Feminism.* New York: Routledge.

Nehring, Christina. 2002. The Vindications: The Moral Opportunism of Feminist Biography. *Harper's Magazine*, February 2002, 60–65.

Orr, Linda. 1992. Outspoken Women and the Rightful Daughter of the Revolution: Madame de Staël's *Considérations sur la Révolution Français*. In *Rebel Daughters: Women and the French Revolution,* eds. Sara E. Melzer and Leslie W. Rabine, 121–136. New York: Oxford University Press.

Patterson, Yolanda. 1986. Simone de Beauvoir and the Demystification of Motherhood. *Yale French Studies* 72:87–105.

Pratt, Mary Louise. 1992. *Imperial Eyes: Travel Writing and Transculturation*. New York: Routledge.

Ravetz, Alison. 1983. The Trivialisation of Mary Wollstonecraft: A Personal and Professional Career Re-vindicated. *Women's Studies International Forum* 6, no. 5:491–99.

Rich, Adrienne. 1976. *Of Woman Born: Motherhood as Experience and Institution*. New York: W. W. Norton.

Riley, Denise. 1988. *Ain't I That Name? Feminism and the Category of "Women" in History*. Minneapolis: University of Minnesota Press.

———. 1992. A Short History of Some Preoccupations. In *Feminists Theorize the Political*, eds. Judith Butler and Joan W. Scott, 121–29. New York: Routledge.

Robinson, Lillian. 1999. Review of *A Transatlantic Love Affair. Women's Review of Books* 16, no. 7:1–4.

Rossi, A. 1995. A Feminist Friendship: Elizabeth Cady Stanton and Susan B. Anthony. In *One Woman, One Vote,* ed. M. Spruill Wheeler, 45–60. Troutdale, OR: NewSage Press.

Rousseau, Jean-Jacques. 1960. *Politics and the Arts: Letter to M. D'Alembert on the Theatre,* trans. Allan Bloom. Ithaca, NY: Cornell University Press.

———. 1979a. *Emile, or on Education*, trans. Allan Bloom. New York: BasicBooks.

———. 1979b. *Reveries of the Solitary Walker*. New York: Penguin.

Sapiro, Virginia. 1992. *A Vindication of Political Virtue: The Political Theory of Mary Wollstonecraft*. Chicago, IL: University of Chicago Press.

———. 1996. Wollstonecraft, Feminism, and Democracy: "Being Bastilled." In *Feminist Interpretations of Mary Wollstonecraft,* ed. Maria J. Falco, 33–45. University Park: Pennsylvania State University Press.

Schwarzer, Alice. 1984. *Conversations with Simone de Beauvoir*. New York: Pantheon.

Scott, Joan. 1988. *Gender and the Politics of History*. New York: Columbia University Press.

———. 1992. Experience. In *Feminists Theorize the Political*, eds. Judith Butler and Joan W. Scott, 22–40. New York: Routledge.

———. 1996. *Only Paradoxes to Offer: French Feminists and the Rights of Man*. Cambridge, MA: Harvard University Press.

Shanley, Mary Lyndon. 1998. Mary Wollstonecraft on Sensibility, Women's Rights, and Patriarchal Power. In *Women Writers and the Early Modern British Political Tradition,* ed. Hilda L. Smith, 148–67. Cambridge, UK: Cambridge University Press.

Sheriff, Mary D. 1996. *The Exceptional Woman: Elisabeth Vigée-Lebrun and the Cultural Politics of Art.* Chicago, IL: University of Chicago Press.

Shulman, A. 1983. Emma Goldman: Anarchist Queen. In *Feminist Theorists: Three Centuries of Key Women Thinkers,* ed. D. Spender, 218–28. New York: Pantheon.

Simons, Margaret A. 1992. Lesbian Connections: Simone de Beauvoir and Feminism. *SIGNS* 18, no. 1:136–61.

———. 1999. *Beauvoir and the Second Sex: Feminism, Race, and the Origins of Existentialism.* New York: Rowman and Littlefield.

Smith, Bonnie. 1996. History and Genius: The Narcotic, Erotic, and Baroque Life of Germaine de Staël. *French Historical Studies* 19, no.4:1059–81.

Spelman, Elizabeth. 1988. *Inessential Woman: Problems of Exclusion in Feminist Thought.* Boston, MA: Beacon Press.

Staël, Germaine de. 1818a. *Considerations on the Principal Events of the French Revolution,* vol. 1. 3 vols. London: Baldwin, Cradock, and Joy.

———. 1818b. *Considerations on the Principal Events of the French Revolution,* vol. 2. 3 vols. London: Baldwin, Cradock, and Joy.

———. 1964. On Literature Considered in Relation to Social Institutions. In *Madame de Staël on Politics, Literature, and National Character,* ed. Morroe Berger, Garden City, NY: Doubleday & Co.

———. 1987. *Corinne, or Italy,* trans. Avriel Goldberger. New Brunswick, NJ: Rutgers University Press.

———. 1995a. *Reflections on the Trial of the Queen, by a Woman.* Appendix B. In Anne A. A. Mini. *An Expressive Revolution.* Ph.D. diss., University of Washington, 365–92.

———. 1995b. *Delphine,* trans. Avriel Goldberger. Dekalb: Northern Illinois University Press, 1995.

———. 2000. *Ten Years of Exile,* trans. Avriel Goldberger. Dekalb: Northern Illinois University Press.

Stansell, Christine. 2000. *American Moderns: Bohemian New York and the Creation of a New Century.* New York: Metropolitan Books.

Steedman, Carolyn Kay. 1986. *Landscape for a Good Woman.* New Brunswick, NJ: Rutgers University Press.

Todd, Janet. 2000. *Mary Wollstonecraft: A Revolutionary Life.* New York: Columbia University Press.

———. ed. 2003. *The Collected Letters of Mary Wollstonecraft.* New York: Columbia University Press.

————, and Marilyn Butler, eds. 1989. *The Works of Mary Wollstonecraft.* 7 vols. New York: New York University Press.

Tomalin, Claire. 1974. *The Life and Death of Mary Wollstonecraft.* New York: Harcourt, Brace, Jovanovich.

Trimberger, E. 1996. Feminism, Men, and Modern Love: Greenwich Village, 1900–1925. In *Powers of Desire: The Politics of Sexuality,* eds. A. Snitow, C. Stansell, and S. Thompson. New York: Monthly Review Press, 1983:131–152.

Vintges, Karen. 1996. *Philosophy as Passion: The Thinking of Simone de Beauvoir.* Bloomington: Indiana University Press.

Walker, Michelle Boulous. 1998. Mother–Daughter Poetics. In *Philosophy and the Maternal Body,* 170–75. New York: Routledge.

Ward, Julie K. 1995. Beauvoir's Two Senses of Body in *The Second Sex.* In *Feminist Interpretations of Simone de Beauvoir,* ed. Margaret A. Simons, 223–42. University Park: Pennsylvania State University Press.

Wardle, Ralph, ed. 1979. *Collected Letters of Mary Wollstonecraft.* Ithaca, NY: Cornell University Press.

Ware, Susan. 2002. *Modern American Women: A Documentary History.* New York: McGraw Hill.

Wells, Ida B. 1970. *Crusade for Justice: The Autobiography of Ida B. Wells,* ed. Alfreda M. Duster. Chicago, IL: University of Chicago Press.

————. 1997. *Southern Horrors and Other Writings: The Anti-Lynching Campaign of Ida B. Wells, 1892–1900,* ed. Jacqueline Joyce Royster. New York: Bedford St. Martin's Press.

Wexler, Alice. 1982. Emma Goldman in Love. *Raritan* 1:116–45.

————. 1984. *Emma Goldman: An Intimate Life.* New York: Pantheon.

————. 1989. *Emma Goldman in Exile: From the Russian Revolution to the Spanish Civil War.* Boston, MA: Beacon Press.

Wheeler, M., ed. 1995. *One Woman, One Vote: Rediscovering the Woman Suffrage Movement.* Troutdale, OR: NewSage Press.

White, Deborah Gray. 1999. *Too Heavy a Load: Black Women in Defense of Themselves, 1894–1994.* New York: W. W. Norton.

Whitford, Margaret. 1991. *Luce Irigaray: Philosophy in the Feminine.* New York: Routledge.

Wiegman, Robyn. 1995. *American Anatomies: Theorizing Race and Gender.* Durham, NC: Duke University Press.

Wollstonecraft, Mary. 1979. *Collected Letters of Mary Wollstonecraft,* ed. R. Wardle. Ithaca, NY: Cornell University Press.

————. 1987. *A Short Residence in Sweden, Norway, and Denmark,* ed. Richard Holmes. New York: Penguin.

————. 1988. *A Vindication of the Rights of Woman,* ed. Carol Poston. New York: W. W. Norton.

————. 1989a. An Historical and Moral Overview of the French Revolution. In *The Works of Mary Wollstonecraft*, vol. 6, eds. Janet Todd and Marilyn Butler. New York: New York University Press.

————. 1989b. *A Vindication of the Rights of Men*. In *The Works of Mary Wollstonecraft*, vol. 5, eds. Janet Todd and Marilyn Butler. New York: New York University Press.

————. 1994. *Maria, or the Wrongs of Woman*. New York: W. W. Norton.

Women's Review of Books. The Memoir Boom. July 13, 1996.

Woodcock, George, ed. 1977. *The Anarchist Reader*. Atlantic Highlands, NY: Humanities Press.

Zerilli, Linda. 2005. *Feminism and the Abyss of Freedom*. Chicago, IL: Chicago University Press.

————. 1989a. An Historical and Moral Overview of the French Revolution. In *The Works of Mary Wollstonecraft*, vol. 6, eds. Janet Todd and Marilyn Butler. New York: New York University Press.

————. 1989b. *A Vindication of the Rights of Men*. In *The Works of Mary Wollstonecraft*, vol. 5, eds. Janet Todd and Marilyn Butler. New York: New York University Press.

————. 1994. *Maria, or the Wrongs of Woman*. New York: W. W. Norton.

Women's Review of Books. The Memoir Boom. July 13, 1996.

Woodcock, George, ed. 1977. *The Anarchist Reader*. Atlantic Highlands, NY: Humanities Press.

Zerilli, Linda. 2005. *Feminism and the Abyss of Freedom*. Chicago, IL: Chicago University Press.

Endnotes

Chapter 1

1   The use of the term *genealogy* refers here to a historical account of earlier feminists that unsettles the prevailing hermeneutic and pluralizes the available narratives. This is not a genealogy of the Foucaultian sort, yet the effect of women acknowledging their location within a female inheritance does serve to disrupt our previous claims to knowledge.

2   See Staël's novels *Delphine* and *Corinne, or Italy.*

Chapter 2

1   After listing a number of rather unattractive characteristics for women such as being "prudent and petty," having no sense of "fact or accuracy," lacking morality, being "contemptibly utilitarian," "false, theatrical, self-seeking, and so on," Beauvoir (1989, 597) admitted "there is an element of truth to all this." But, she added, "we must only note that the varieties of behavior reported are not dictated to woman by her hormones nor predetermined in the structure of the female brain: they are shaped as in a mold by her situation."

2   For an extended discussion of Wollstonecraft's and Staël's writings on these questions, see Marso (2002).

3   See Marso (1999) for an extended discussion of how women's desire disrupts and refashions the public sphere.

4   Northern states passed literacy requirements, and southern states disenfranchised blacks through their constitutions.

Chapter 3

1   Though Beauvoir did not claim to be a feminist in 1949 when writing *The Second Sex,* feminists claim her as a founding feminist. Indeed, chapter 6 explores feminists' relationship to Beauvoir as feminist mother.

2   In *The Ethics of Ambiguity*, Beauvoir (1976, 156) argued that the individual "is
     defined only by his relationship to the world and to other individuals; he exists only
     by transcending himself, and his freedom can be achieved only through the free-
     dom of others." I explore this quote further later in this chapter.

3   Lila Abu-Lughod (2002, 787) helpfully delineated what she saw as the difference
     between the "hard work involved in recognizing and respecting differences" versus
     being "cultural relativists who respect whatever goes on elsewhere as 'just their
     culture.'"

4   In her work on Kant's *Critique of Judgment*, Hannah Arendt (1982, 84) referred to
     "the example" as a philosophical category. Arendt argued that the example could
     "lead and guide us, and the judgment thus acquires exemplary validity." According
     to Arendt (1997), exploring the life of Rahel Varnhagen, for example, illustrates
     more than her singular life: It illuminates her situation as a woman, a Jewess, her
     attempts at assimilation, and her acts of revolt. Also see Zerilli (2005) for an illumi-
     nating discussion of how feminists might employ Arendt's concept of judging.

Chapter 4

1   The Girondins were members of the moderate Republican Party, so called because
     a number of its leaders came from the Gironde region of southwestern France. They
     controlled the Legislative Assembly from late 1791 to late 1792 but were ousted by
     the radical Montagnards under Jean-Paul Marat in 1793. Many Girondin leaders
     were executed during the Reign of Terror.

2   While pregnant with her second daughter, who would become Mary Wollstonecraft
     Godwin Shelley, Wollstonecraft married radical author William Godwin in March
     1797. Wollstonecraft died in September 1797 after giving birth to this child.
     Soon after, Godwin published his tribute to her, titled *Memoirs of the Author of
     the Rights of Woman*. Wendy Gunther-Canada (2001) warns against reliance on
     Godwin's biography of Mary Wollstonecraft. She argues, "The danger of Godwin's
     revisionist biography is that it reinscribes Rousseau's gender binary that men are
     born to think and women are born to feel and thus undermines the very premise
     of Wollstonecraft's political project—specifically, that in a democratic age reason
     should rule, and since women are rational beings they are capable of governing
     themselves" (p. 165). Gunther-Canada, overall, is highly critical of studies that
     link Wollstonecraft's biography with her theory; she is even wary of an empha-
     sis on Wollstonecraft's novels, reminding us that Wollstonecraft was a "lifelong
     critic of the novel" (p. 157) because it appealed to the cult of feminine sensibility.
     Alison Ravetz (1983) would agree with Gunther-Canada (2001) in the assessment
     that Godwin's memoir and its emphasis on Wollstonecraft's private life belittles
     Wollstonecraft's contribution to feminist theory. Mitzi Myers's (1981, 300) assess-
     ment, alternatively, offers a scholarly examination of how Godwin's (1987) memoir
     "unites Wollstonecraft's notion of herself, Godwin's reading of her character, and
     his analysis of that character's impact on himself and his philosophy." Myers (1981,
     309) concludes that every scholar needs to decide how to "resolve the complexities

of her [Wollstonecraft's] character and achievement, how to adjust her rationalism and her romanticism." While it is true that Godwin's biography does indeed high-light Wollstonecraft's life and loves—even her sexuality—I contend that the reading of Godwin's memoir along with Wollstonecraft's own letters and autobiographical work helps us, as contemporary feminists, to understand the complexity of her life and work, including her deep ambivalence regarding feminine sensibility. This should work to enhance her feminism and to enable a deeper appreciation of her legacy.

3   The dominant view expressed by those who study Wollstonecraft's political work is that she was a woman of reason. Mary Lyndon Shanley (1998, 150) writes, for example, that Wollstonecraft felt "exaggerated notions of female sensibility cor-rupted both women and men, and worked against the extension of fundamental rights of citizenship to women." See Jacobus (1995), Favret (1993), Myers (1979), and Moskal (1991) for literary studies of Wollstonecraft's letters and novel.

4   For example, of the *Letters from Sweden*, Virginia Sapiro (1992, 35–36) wrote, "The letters do not mark as radical a departure as some have suggested. This Romanticism does not make her a sighing, swooning creature. Rather, she is the sol-itary walker of her much-beloved *Reveries of the Solitary Walker.* She well understood that if a male solitary walker needed inner strength to carry him on his journey and allow him to struggle with his nature, a woman needed much more. She had by no means lost her respect for reason or her search for virtue."

5   See Kelly (1996) and Todd (2000) for recent analyses that link Wollstonecraft's life and experiences to her theory.

6   Todd (2000, 242) documents that nearly 35,000 people met their death in the Great Terror.

7   Wollstonecraft was employed as Imlay's legal representative to investigate the disap-pearance of one of his cargo ships loaded with French silver. Imlay suspected foul play; Wollstonecraft undertook this dangerous voyage in an attempt to discover the circumstances of the boat's disappearance.

Chapter 5

1   Goldman was deported, along with 248 other immigrants, in September 1919 after serving two years in prison for opposing the World War I draft. She lost her citizen-ship on a technicality. The government denaturalized her former husband and by law at that time a woman's citizenship followed her husband's.

2   Since the 1917 Revolution, Goldman and Berkman had thought about going back to their home country but their political work in the United States, as well as a genuine commitment to the United States on Goldman's part, precluded them from making the move.

3   Upon deportation to Soviet Russia, Goldman and Berkman refused to toe the Communist Party line on the Soviet Union's potential for human emancipation. Though they had fully supported the Revolution from abroad, witnessing Soviet

repression of political dissidents sobered their early enthusiasm. Goldman's exposé of Soviet brutality in *My Disillusionment in Russia*, published in 1923, incurred the wrath of radicals around the world.

4   Goldman (1970c, 555) called homosexuality the "problem most tabooed in polite society." Over the objections of many of her anarchist comrades, Goldman often spoke on the theme of prejudice against homosexuality on her lecture tours. Blanche Weisen Cook (1977, 56) argued that though Goldman felt "a profound ambivalence about lesbianism as a lifestyle" she was "the only woman in America who defended homosexuality...and was absolute about a person's right to sexual choice." Jonathan Ned Katz (1992, 523) included excerpts from fascinating letters from Almeda Sperry, an anarchist colleague, to Goldman; he argued that it is "difficult to know exactly what occurred between Sperry and Goldman," but the letters from Sperry leave no doubt as to her romantic and sexual feelings for Goldman. If Goldman had a lesbian affair with Sperry, she did not acknowledge this in her own autobiography, nor did she theorize its importance in terms of her own divergence from hetero-sexual norms. Goldman did, however, openly support homosexual desire and free expression of sexuality.

5   "Without a history, political movements like ours swing back and forth endlessly, reacting to earlier mistakes and overreacting in compensation, unable to incorporate previous insights and transcend previous limitations" (DuBois and Gordon 1983, 8). For an historical perspective on the debates surrounding sexuality in Emma Goldman's time, see DuBois and Gordon.

6   Women in the American suffrage movement exhibited a wide range of political perspectives on the singular importance of the vote over the seventy-five years they struggled to achieve their goal. Even Susan B. Anthony and Elizabeth Cady Stanton, the early pioneers, differed regarding women's rights beyond suffrage. For a fascinating discussion regarding how personal circumstances and family back-grounds might have affected these women's political perspectives, see Rossi (1995).

7   This was more acute since many of the anarchist colleagues whom Goldman most respected, Berkman included, did not feel that Reitman was politically committed to the cause and treated him as peripheral, merely Emma's lover.

8   Marsh (1981, 172) noted that de Cleyre, an important anarchist feminist and friend of Goldman's, ended an important relationship because she felt unable to conquer her possessiveness.

Chapter 6

1   As Irigaray (1993b, 108) argues, "This world of female ethics would continue to have two vertical and horizontal dimensions: Daughter-to-mother, mother-to-daughter; among women, or among 'sisters.' In some way, the vertical dimension is always being taken away from female becoming. The bond between mother and daughter, daughter and mother, has to be broken for the daughter to become a woman. Female genealogy has to be suppressed, on behalf of the son-father relation-

ship, and the idealization of the father and husband as patriarchs. But without a vertical dimension…a loving ethical order cannot take place among women."

2   Beauvoir (1984) made the case that circumstances of an individual life necessarily illuminate the lives of others. She said she wanted to describe the realization of her "vocation as a writer," arguing that the "individual case" reveals much more than "generalized abstractions" (p. 9).

3   *The Women's Review of Books* (1996, 5) chronicles an "avalanche of published memoirs by women in recent years."

4   Debates within contemporary feminism raise questions concerning the political as well as the philosophical risks of speaking of *women* as a coherent identity. Elizabeth Spelman (1988, 3) identified the political paradox at the heart of feminism: "Any attempt to talk about all women in terms of something we have in common undermines the attempt to talk about the differences among us, and vice versa. Is it possible to give the things women have in common their full significance without thereby implying that the differences among us are less important? How can we describe those things that differentiate women without eclipsing what we share in common?"

5   Beauvoir (1989) explained in *The Second Sex* that to desire is man's domain as subject: Woman is merely the object of his attention (see especially ch. 14, "Sexual Initiation"). Here Beauvoir offered numerous examples of how men and women differently experience the sexual act. The man is the "subject as opposed to objects that he perceives and instruments he manipulates; he projects himself toward the other without losing his independence; the feminine flesh is for him a prey" (p. 371).

6   Of this scene Toril Moi writes that "her exceptional position as a woman who can deal with men on an equal footing, that is to say without making them feel ill at ease, is confirmed when Gerbert compares her to one of the boys.…Such a discursive position puts her in a double bind, preventing her at once from flirting like a female and from speaking (or grabbing hands) like a man" (1994, 137–38).

7   For studies that focus on Beauvoir's ethics as related to her emphasis on love and sexual desire see Bergoffen (1997) and Vintges (1996). A focus on Beauvoir's sexuality is also central to the collection edited by Hawthorne (2000).

8   Since the 1970s, feminists have thought about the implications of theorizing from the perspective of the varieties of feminine desire. What would the world look like if the Other (as Beauvoir described it) or the unsignifiable (in Irigaray's sense) would speak in the language of her own desire? (see De Lauretis 1994 and Milan Women's Bookstore Collective 1990). Feminists from the Milan Women's Bookstore Collective (1990, 115) assert that for philosophers and politicians within the tradition extolling the universality of civil, human, and individual rights, "female difference is indecent." As Beauvoir (1989, 3) noted, "The term 'female' is derogatory not because it emphasizes women's animality, but because it imprisons her in her sex." It comes as no surprise, then, that a woman encounters real difficulty "acknowledging the immensity of a [sexual] desire she has no way of putting forward, openly, in

full sight of society, without the disguise of some female virtue" (Milan Women's Bookstore Collective, 1990, 115).

9   Beauvoir (1989, 645) wrote in *The Second Sex*, "It is man's good fortune—in adult-hood as in early childhood—to be obliged to take the most arduous roads, but the surest; it is woman's misfortune to be surrounded by almost irresistible temptations; everything incites her to follow the easy slopes; instead of being invited to fight her own way up, she is told that she has only to let herself slide and she will attain paradises of enchantment. When she perceives that she has been duped by a mere mirage, it is too late; her strength has been exhausted in a losing venture."

10 In her analysis of her identity as a "third-world feminist," Narayan (1997) stressed the importance of understanding our relationships to our mothers and our mother-cultures in the struggle for feminist consciousness. She wrote, "For many of us, women in different parts of the world, our relationship to our mothers resemble our relationships to the motherlands of the cultures in which we were raised. Both our mothers and our mother-cultures give us all sorts of contradictory messages, encouraging their daughters to be confident, impudent, and self-assertive even as they attempt to instill conformity, decorum, and silence, seemingly oblivious to these contradictions" (p. 8). To achieve feminist consciousness, one must be willing to acknowledge this ambivalence and rewrite our own stories. "Feminist daughters often have accounts of their mother cultures that differ in significant ways from the culture's own dominant account of itself.…Re-telling the story of a mother-culture in feminist terms…is a political enterprise" (p. 10).

11 Kristana Arp (1995) and Julia K. Ward (1995) have claimed that Beauvoir's seem-ingly negative remarks about female biology have been misinterpreted. See their essays in *Feminist Interpretations of Simone de Beauvoir* for a context describing the negative interpretations of Beauvoir's work on female biology as well as an alterna-tive interpretation, one with which I agree, emphasizing Merleau-Ponty's influence on Beauvoir's development of the concept of the female body as a situation.

Chapter 7

1   See for instance, the variety of meanings accorded to the "chador" in the women's magazine, *Zanan*, an Iranian publication founded and published by Shala Sherkat. I was able to examine numerous issues of *Zanan* following a presentation by Shala Haeri, from Boston University, who spoke about *Zanan* and the work of Shala Sherkat as a keynote speaker at the "Women from Iraq and Iran: Visionaries for Peace in the 21st Century Conference," at Westfield State College in Westfield, MA, part of the Global Women's History Project, April 14–17, 2005. Shahla Haeri is author of *No Shame for the Sun: Lives of Professional Pakistani Women* (Syracuse University Press in the U.S. and Oxford University Press in Pakistan, 2002).

2   See Hirschmann (2003) for extended discussions on the construction of desires and the possibility of free choice. Her analysis complements my reading of Beauvoir.

Index